THE LORD'S SUPPER FROM WYCLIFFE TO CRANMER

The Lord's Supper

from

Wycliffe to Cranmer

DAVID BROUGHTON KNOX

Exeter
The Paternoster Press

AUSTRALIA:
Bookhouse Australia Ltd.,
P.O. Box 115, Flemington Markets, NSW 2129

SOUTH AFRICA:
Oxford University Press,
P.O. Box 1141, Cape Town

British Library Cataloguing in Publication Data

Knox, B. D.
    The Lord's supper from Wycliffe to Cranmer.
    1. Lord's Supper—History
    I. Title
    265'.3'09   BV823

ISBN 0-85364-379-2

Photoset in Great Britain by
Nuprint Services Ltd, Harpenden, Herts.
and printed for The Paternoster Press.
Paternoster House, 3 Mount Radford Crescent, Exeter, Devon
by A. Wheaton & Co., Ltd., Exeter

Contents

TO THE STUDENTS OF MOORE COLLEGE

Preface

It is almost six hundred years since John Wycliffe died on December 31, 1394. He was a man of great and original intellect who 'anticipated a reform of Christianity more pure than the genius of Protestantism of the sixteenth century could attain', as his nineteenth century biographer and editor Robert Vaughan put it (*Tracts & Treatises of John de Wycliffe*, p xcii).

This book focuses on one important aspect of Wycliffe's teaching and seeks to show that his doctrine of the Lord's Supper had a continuous history among Wycliffe's followers in England until it was incorporated into the English Prayer Books of Edward VI.

I am grateful to the Evangelical Library for permission to incorporate in it parts of my Evangelical Library Lecture.

John Wycliffe

John Wycliffe was the first Englishman to teach clearly and fully the Reformed doctrine on the Lord's Supper.

Wycliffe was born about 1325 or 1330. He went up to Oxford round the age of fifteen, and in due course became the leading intellectual in the university and in Europe. His most characteristic contribution to scholastic thought during the time of his heyday at Oxford was his development of Archbishop Fitzralph's doctrine of dominion, namely, that dominion, of which God is the only source, can be exercised rightly only on God's behalf. Wycliffe based his doctrine of dominion on grace rather than on creation and this led him to conclude that dominion and lordship can be rightly exercised only by those in a state of grace. Moreover, it did not belong to spiritual persons, the clergy and bishops, to exercise dominion at all, for christ gave his church authority over the spiritual, not the temporal realm. Wycliffe therefore advocated the disendowing of the church and argued that the territorial church should be governed by the king. Not surprisingly, these views brought him into conflict with church authorities. He was expelled from Oxford in 1378 and retired to Lutterworth, of which he was the parson. He died six years later. It was while in retirement at Lutterworth that Wycliffe developed and promulgated his distinctive teaching on the Lord's Supper.

Wycliffe fully merits the title of 'The morning star of the

Reformation', which a later generation conferred on him. The formal principle of the Reformation is the unique supremacy of scripture. Others before Wycliffe had stressed the supremacy of scripture but had regarded the scriptures and the teachings of the church as co-ordinate, scripture and church dogma speaking with one voice. This is also the view of the post-tridentine Roman Catholic church. But Wycliffe and the Reformers were of the opinion that observation showed the facts to be otherwise and that in truth the teaching of scripture and the current teaching of the church were in certain points in conflict. Two conclusions followed—one that the church's teaching could be in error, and the other that church teaching and church institutions should be corrected and reformed by the teaching of scripture.

The church can err

Wycliffe applied this principle in his treatment of the Lord's Supper in the treatise *De Eucharistia* which he wrote in 1380. He begins with an attack on the doctrine of transubstantiation, which had been made *de fide* by the Fourth Lateran Council in 1215. He cites the confession of Berengar, made to a Roman synod in the eleventh century, to the effect that 'the same bread and wine which were placed before the mass upon the altar remain after the consecration both as sacrament and as the Lord's body' and concludes from this 'that it was once the meaning of the church, as an article of faith, that bread and wine remained after consecration of the Eucharist just as before.' Since, however, transubstantiation contradicts this, Wycliffe deduces: 'From this it is clear that the Roman church can err in articles of faith, since it has so done. Secondly, it is clear that it is not necessary to believe that if the Roman Church declares anything Catholic or heretical, it therefore does so truly.'[1]

Without scriptural foundations

Wycliffe's next point is that transubstantiation is without scriptural foundation. 'No one ought to believe even the pope

10

in matters of faith except to the extent that his pronouncements are founded on scripture. But neither upon scripture nor reason nor revelation can the Avignonese (i.e. papal) church base the said transubstantiation.'[2]

Wycliffe was convinced that transubstantiation contradicted scripture, for the scriptures affirm that the bread remains after the consecration of the eucharist. In *Trialogus,* one of his last books, he pointed out that in our Lord's words 'This is my body', the pronoun 'this' can refer only to bread. 'For the sacramental words had not yet been uttered that it should cease to be bread.'[3] It is bread, therefore, which Christ says is his body. That the bread remains after the consecration is confirmed by the fact that

> the apostles recognized Christ with breaking of bread, as we are told in Luke xxiv. And Augustine, with the papal enactment, De Con. Dist. III. *non omnes,* tells us that this bread is this venerable sacrament. Or are we to doubt its following, that the apostles having known Christ in the breaking of this bread, therefore that seeming bread must have been bread? Our apostle, likewise, who takes his meaning from our Lord, calls this sacrament the bread which we break, as is manifest in 1 Cor. x., and often again in the following chapter. Who then would venture to blaspheme God, by maintaining that so chosen a vessel could apply erroneous terms to the chief of the sacraments—especially with the foreknowledge that heresies would take their rise from that very subject? It is impossible to believe that Paul would have been so careless of the church, the spouse of Christ, as so frequently to have called this sacrament bread, and not by its real name, had he known that it was not bread, but an accident without a subject; and when he was besides aware, by the gift of prophecy, of all the future heresies which men would entertain on the matter.[4]

Irrationality

Wycliffe objected to the irrationality of transubstantiation. It teaches that the sacrament consists of accidents without substance which Wycliffe scornfully rejects as meaningless. It involves God the Creator destroying his innocent creation, for the bread is turned into nothing. 'For they say that in the consecration of their host, they bless the bread and wine so that it becomes nothing, since according to their doctrine no part of it remains in the body of Christ, or in his sacrament, but...it is annihilated and turned into nothing...yet Christ, since it is his own workmanship, preserves it!'[5]

Since transubstantiation is so contrary to the senses it is unworthy of God, since 'without good reason, it not only destroys guiltless existence, but it puts confusion on that intellect which He has implanted in our nature.'[6]

It also nullifies our faculty of judgement. Though the consecrated hosts are Christ and unconsecrated hosts remain bread, yet they are indistinguishable and therefore indiscernable as to whether consecrated or not. Wycliffe comments: 'What could move our Lord Jesus Christ thus to take away the power of judgement from his worshippers?;[7] 'Mice, however, have an innate knowledge of the fact, that the substance of bread is retained, as at first; but these unbelievers have no such knowledge, since they know not what bread or what wine are consecrated, except they have seen the act of consecration performed.'[8]

Worse than pagans

The practical objection which Wycliffe had to transubstantiation was that it led directly to idolatry. 'Too many laymen as well as clergy are so unfaithful in this matter that they believe, worse than pagans, that the consecrated host is their God.' Pagans at least believe that their idols consist of their natural substance, wood or stone, as well as partaking of deity. But not so the transubstantiationist. As a consequence this doctrine of transubstantiation distorts a Christian's understanding of the Trinity as well as of the Incarnation.[9]

Wycliffe's positive teaching

In his positive exposition of the meaning of the Lord's Supper Wycliffe anticipated with clarity and fulness the doctrine of the Swiss and English Reformation, taught on the Continent by Zwingli and Calvin and in England by Frith,

Joye, Tyndale and Cranmer and which was incorporated in the two Edwardian Prayer Books. It is an interesting aspect of the Reformation that Luther's theory of the Lord's Supper made no appeal in England. English Reformed theology was from the beginning and without deviation unambiguously 'Reformed' (or 'Zwinglian', to concede a term used exclusively by opponents of this doctrine).

The pedigree of ideas is not always easy to trace; but there is no reason to doubt that the English doctrine of the Lord's Supper derives directly from Wycliffe through Lollardy. *Trialogus,* one of the last books Wycliffe wrote, contains a clear exposition of the doctrine of the Lord's Supper at which he had arrived in his last years of life and which would also be the doctrine which he taught his Lollard preachers whom he organised during these last years at Lutterworth. Wycliffe may also have influenced the English Reformed doctrine of the sacrament by his contribution to the shaping of Swiss concepts of the Lord's Supper, either indirectly through Hussite admiration for his teaching or directly through the Swiss Reformers acquaintance with his writings. It is well known that Huss valued Wycliffe's writings and translated many of them into Czech, including the *Trialogus.* The *Trialogus* was also known directly to the Swiss Reformers. It was printed in Basle as early as March 7, 1525 and it is interesting to note that it was the first of a long list of proscribed books described as having been imported into London, in a proclamation of 1529. In this proclamation the *Trialogus* is designated in the following unexpected terms:

Johannis Wycleffi viri piissimi Dialogorum libri quatuor, quorum primus divinitatem et ideas tractat: secundus, rerum universarum creationem complectitur: tertius, de virtutibus vitiisque ipsis contrariis copiossissime loquitur: quartus, Romanae Ecclesiae Sacramenta, ejus pestiferam dotationem, Antichristi Regnum, Fratrum fraudulentam originem atque eorum hypocrisim demonstrat.[10]

(Four books of Dialogues, by the very religious man John Wycliffe. The first deals with Deity and Ideas, the second covers the creation of the universe, the third speaks fully of the virtues and their corresponding vices, the fourth describes the sacraments of the Roman church, its pernicious endowment, the reign of Anti Christ, the false origins of the friars and their hypocrisy.)

This designation was taken from the printed title page and reflects the Swiss Reformers' view of Wycliffe. Its printing in Basle in 1525 makes it the first book written by an Englishman to be printed, which expounds these doctrines. Its proscription in 1529 shows that the printed edition was being circulated in England. Young English Reformation scholars like John Frith would be acquainted with Wycliffe's views directly from this book as well as indirectly through Lollard tradition and such Lollard tracts circulating in manuscript as *Wycliffe's wicket.*

Wycliffe began his exposition of the Lord's Supper in the *Trialogus* by affirming emphatically that 'this sacrament is the body of Christ in the form of bread'.[11]

'Christ, who cannot lie, said that the bread that he held in his hands was really his body.'[12] The bread is Christ's body by way of sacrament or figure. Thus in *The Eucharist* he wrote: 'When we see the host we ought to believe not that it is itself the body of Christ, but that the body of Christ is sacramentally concealed in it.'[13] (Sacramentally means by way of sign, i.e figuratively.) Christ called the bread his body by way of a figure or simile, just as he called John the Baptist Elijah. Wycliffe wrote in these terms in *The Eucharist* (4:2) and repeated them in *Trialogus.*

Do we believe...that John the Baptist, who was made by the word of Christ to be Elias (Mt. xi) ceased to be John or ceased to be anything that he was substantially before? In the same manner, accordingly, though the bread becomes the body of Christ, by nature of his words, it need not cease to be bread. For it is bread substantially, after it has begun to be sacramentally the body of Christ. For thus saith Christ, "This is my body", and in consequence this must be admitted, like the assertion in the eleventh chapter of the gospel of Matthew, about the Baptist, "And if ye will receive it, this is Elias." And Christ does not, to avoid equivocation, contradict the Baptist when he declares, "I

14

am not Elias". The one meaning that he was Elias figuratively, the other that he was not Elias personally. And in the same manner it is merely a double meaning and not a contradiction, in those who admit that this sacrament is not naturally the body of Christ but that this sacrament is Christ's body figuratively.[14]

Wycliffe returned again to the same illustration to explain the nature of Christ's body in the sacrament. His interlocutor asked: 'There is one thing I would fain know, and that is, in what sense the bread is the body of the Lord, and yet not identically the very body?' Wycliffe replied:

As to the mode in which the bread is the body of our Lord, such it surely is—believe this firmly, for Christ who cannot lie has so said. Now you know there are three methods of prediction—the formal, the essential and the figurative. Passing by the two former let us attend to the third. It is according to the third mode that Christ calls John the Baptist Elias.

Like Tyndale later, Wycliffe went on to affirm that this style of language is frequent in Scripture. Thus Christ is called a rock in 1 Corinthians 10,

and in Genesis 41 the Scripture asserts that seven ears of corn and seven fat cows are seven years. And as Augustine observes, the Scripture does not say—are the signs of those years, but are the years themselves. You will meet with such modes of expression constantly in scripture. Now all such expressions show that the thing (res) of the subject is ordained by God to be the figure of the thing of the predicate.[15]

Those heretics are not to be listened to, who endeavour to do away with the meaning thus assigned, by the false objection, that such a figurative mode of expression is not used on any other occasion in the gospel. for in Luke 22 it is immediately subjoined, "Do this in remembrance of me;" as if it had been said—This sacramental bread should be taken as an efficient memorial of me. Paul (1 Cor. 11) speaks in a similar manner— "this cup," etc., where there can be no doubt of its being a figurative expression; since in Mark 14 Christ saith, "This is my blood," etc., where the words show the same thing; for the mind of the Catholic cannot comprehend that the bread is the body of

Christ, except by a figurative understanding of these words; inasmuch as to identify these two things is impossible. Beyond all doubt, then, the expression "this is my body", is figurative, as are those in the gospel of John: "unless ye eat the flesh of the Son of man", with many like them, which Christ spake in another sense. Nevertheless, there are some expressions in Scripture which must be understood plainly and without figure, as we grant in the matter of the incarnation.[16]

A Reformed understanding?

Exponents of the Reformed doctrine of the Lord's Supper are liable to be misapprehended by their commentators on account of the fact that they affirm with our Lord that the bread is his body. But there are three simple tests to discover whether a writer is expounding Reformed doctrine or not. Does he disassociate our Lord's real presence in the Supper from a local presence with the bread and wine; does he in the context of the Supper think of our Lord's body as in heaven; does he deny that 'the wicked and those devoid of a lifely faith' partake of Christ's body?[17] On each of these three questions Wycliffe stands with the English and Swiss Reformers, in contrast to the Lutherans and the Tridentines.

Thus Wycliffe affirmed that our Lord's body is not to be locally associated with the bread and wine. Each piece of the broken bread of the Eucharist 'is not really but figuratively the body of the Lord... Therefore there is no need that a thing made by God thus symbolically, should stand in any need of the presence of the thing of which it is the figure; or that the thing itself, of which it is the figure, should be locally approximated to it.'[18]

Secondly, Wycliffe affirmed quite clearly that in the context of the Lord's Supper, Christ's body is to be thought of as really in heaven. In *The Eucharist,* he affirmed: 'That which is in heaven is really the body of Christ.'[19]... 'The body of Christ is in heaven.'[20] In the *Trialogus* he wrote: 'The body of the Lord is above', and, 'It is not to be understood that the body of Christ descends to the host in any church where it is being consecrated but remains above the skies, stable and unmoved.' Wycliffe added that in a sense the body of Christ is present everywhere, pervading the world, in a spiritual and virtual manner; and in the host the body of Christ is particularly present, 'since it is the host itself figuratively.'[21]

Thirdly, Wycliffe affirmed in *The Eucharist* that the wicked and those devoid of a lively faith do not partake of the body of Christ, but only of the sacrament, that is to say the sign, of the body of Christ. (The words *sign* and *sacrament* are synonymous). 'Neither a beast, (e.g. a mouse) nor a man eternally foreknown to be reprobate eats Christ's body with his teeth though he corporally chews the sacrament.'[22] Wycliffe quoted the passage from Augustine which was later incorporated in the twenty-ninth of the Thirty-nine Articles and commented:

> the wonderful subtlety of the words of the doctor is clear in which he says, not that an unworthy person visibly presses the body of Christ with his teeth but that he visibly presses the sacrament of the body and blood of Christ with his teeth. For that sacrament ought specially to be distinguished from the body of Christ which is the matter of the sacrament thereof.[23]

There are five concepts which are characteristic of the English Reformation doctrine of the Lord's supper, the concepts of 'double eating', of the eye of faith, of the efficacious sign, of the union of the worshipper with Christ, and of the preaching and praise of God's goodness in Christ being the sacrifice we offer. All five concepts are found in Wycliffe.

1. In addition to the physical eating of the sacrament there is a spiritual eating through the mind. 'In carnal eating that which is eaten changes into nourishment for the eater when it is taken in by his members. But in spiritual eating it is otherwise. When one eats the body of Christ spiritually one is thereby incorporated into the members of the church and thus into Christ.'[24] 'Spiritual receiving of the body of Christ does not consist in bodily receiving the consecrated host but in the feeding of the soul out of the fruitful faith according to which our spirit is nourished in the Lord.'[25] This spiritual eating may be independent of the sacrament. 'Spiritual eating consists in the pious and gracious consideration of how

Christ suffered for the human race.'[26]

2. Faith is the means through which we receive the body of Christ. It is the eye of the soul. 'We distinguish two kinds of seeing, of eating and digesting, namely the corporal and spiritual. We do not see the body of Christ in that sacrament with the bodily eye but rather with the eye of the mind, that is, in faith.'[27]

'When we see the host we ought to believe not that it is itself the body of Christ but that the body of Christ is sacramentally concealed in it.'[28] In the *Trialogus*, Wycliffe repeated the sentiment that it is only through the believer's faith moulded by love that the sacrament is eaten spiritually.[29]

3. Wycliffe anticipated the Thirty-nine Articles in applying the concept of efficacious sign to the bread and wine. 'We priests make and bless the consecrated host, which is not the Lord's body but an efficacious sign thereof.'[30] 'It is certain that so long as the bread remains it is not really the body of Christ but the efficacious sign thereof.'[31] 'It is an efficacious sign to call to memory the life of Christ.'[32] (I.e. it is efficacious for this purpose.)

4. Furthermore, 'The host is a sign, among other things, of the union of Christ and his church.'[33]

5. The true worship of God is not in rites and ceremonies, or in the adoration of the host, but in the preaching of God's goodness in Christ and in thanksgiving for this. The sacrifice of the mass consists of praise and thanksgiving for Christ's death. In this, again, Wycliffe anticipated the Reformation. He wrote: 'We sacrifice Christ and offer him to God the Father' in the sacrament 'when we praise and spread abroad the holiness and blessedness which God has instituted in the body of Christ.'[34]

The Reformers emphasised that the sacrament was a sign of the covenant, made on the basis of Christ's death, and pointing to the promises which God had made for us in the gospel and in particular to the promise of the forgiveness of sins. Wycliffe's thought is congruous with these concepts, but he does not explicitly use this language. Through the sacrament the believer is joined to Christ. 'The end of the sacrament is for Christ to dwell in the soul through virtues.'[35]

Since the sacrament is a sign of the gospel, it is not absolutely necessary. On this, the Reformers were explicit,[36] and although Wycliffe does not say so, his language implies it. Thus for the priest, 'uprightly to meditate upon Christ... is infinitely better than to celebrate the sacrament.'[37] Similarly: 'The layman, mindful of the body of Christ in heaven, more efficaciously and in a better manner than this priest who performs the sacrament, yet with equal truth (but in another manner) causes the body of Christ to be with him.'[38]

In one point, however, Wycliffe differed from later orthodox reformed theology, and was—we may think—nearer to the truth. He insisted that the piety of the priest affected the efficacy of the sacrament. 'Since the host is a sign amongst other things of the union of Christ with the church' it is more efficacious as a sign of this when it is consecrated by a man who is himself in union with Christ.[39]

In this Wycliffe was nearer to the truth of the matter than were the Reformers. He understood the Lord's Supper as a sign of fellowship—of the union of Christ with his church; it was an efficacious sign expressing and creating this fellowship. It stands to reason that if the minister of this fellowship with Christ is himself out of fellowship with Christ the fellowship around the sign is greatly lessened if not rendered altogether impossible.

Early Lollards

Walter Brute

Wycliffe died in 1384. In 1391 a Welshman, Walter Brute, was tried by the Bishop of Hereford for heresy concerning the Lord's Supper. Amongst other things he was accused of teaching 'that every Christian man, yea and woman, being without sin, may make the body of Christ as well as the priest. Item, the same Walter has notoriously openly and publically avouched and taught, that in the sacrament of the altar there is not the very body but a sign and memorial only.'[49]

Brute was a layman, a graduate of Oxford and a resident of the diocese of Hereford. The bishop complained that for some time he had been 'teaching openly and privately the nobility as well as the commons' his heresies. He was a friend of William Swinderby, a priest who had been condemned by the bishop earlier in the same month as a preacher 'of the new sect, vulgarly called Lollards.'[41] At his trial Brute handed to the Bishop several lengthy 'declarations' setting out his beliefs. In them he dealt with the doctrine of the Lord's supper.

He based his exposition on John 6 (this became a regular feature in later Lollard doctrine on the sacrament and is interesting as Wycliffe had implied that John 6 did not refer to the sacrament). Consequently he connected the eating of

Christ's body closely with faith in Christ's incarnation and in his death for our redemption. To believe these truths is to eat and drink Christ's flesh and blood. 'Like as we do believe by our faith that he is true God, so must we believe that he is true man and then do we eat the bread of heaven and the flesh of Christ and if we believe that he did voluntarily shed his blood for our redemption, then do we drink his blood.'[42] Both in this world and in the next our souls live by feeding on Christ, human and divine. The sacrament of the body and blood of Christ has been given to us to put us in mind of this spiritual meal.

Brute is one of the few who saw in the sacrament an eschatological dimension. Not only is it a sign of feeding on Christ now by faith, but also of our heavenly relationship with Him when our corporal and spiritual natures will be fully refreshed and satisfied through beholding Christ's humanity and deity in heaven. 'And in memory of this double refection, present in this world and in the world to come has Christ given unto us, for eternal blessedness the sacrament of his body and blood in the substance of bread and wine.'[43]

Wycliffe had argued very strongly the rational absurdity of transubstantiation. Brute, however, though conscious of this, rests his objection on its lack of scriptural basis. He was willing to accept gladly that whatever Christ said was true; but he did not believe that Christ's words implied either the concepts of either transubstantiation or consubstantiation. He admitted the possibility of both concepts. Christ could have transubstantiated the bread into his body as he transubstantiated the water into wine; or again, just as he became both God and man, so he could have made the bread 'to be his body really, the bread still remaining as it was before.... He that could make one man to be very God and very man, could, if he would, make one thing to be very bread and his very body. But I do not find it expressly in the Scripture, that he would have any such identity or conjunction to be made'.[44] In the opening paragraph of his declaration, Brute had already made it clear to the bishop that he would be guided in matters of Christian doctrine only 'by the authority of the sacred Scripture or by probable reason grounded on the sacred

Scripture', words which later found an echo in Article 6 of the Thirty-nine Articles.

Brute expounded the Lord's Supper in terms of 'double eating', a concept much used later by the English Reformers, especially by Cranmer. Brute explained to the bishop of Hereford: 'The bread was eaten with the disciples' mouths, that he being the true bread of the soul might be in spirit received and eaten spiritually by their faith who believed in him...The consecrated bread is really bread, as it was before, and yet figuratively the body of Christ.'[45]

In 1395, when Parliament had been convened at Westminster a document containing twelve heads for the reformation of the church was posted on the door of St. Paul's Cathedral and also at Westminster and was later debated in Parliament. However, the king was opposed and nothing was done. The fourth item concerned the Lord's Supper. The *Trialogus* of Wycliffe, (named in the document 'the Evangelical doctor') was quoted as a true exposition of the Sacrament and it was asserted that every godly man and woman may celebrate the sacrament. Anticipating the Black Rubric of the Prayer Book, these members of Parliament affirmed that 'Christ's body is never out of heaven' and denounced transubstantiation as 'a feigned miracle', leading to idolatry.[46]

William Sautry

In 1401 a priest, William Sautry, was examined by Thomas Arundel, the Archbishop of Canterbury, on eight indictments which reflect Lollard teaching, such as saying that it was wrong to worship the cross and that preaching was a better occupation of the time of a priest than saying the daily offices. The last indictment concerned the affirmation 'that after the pronouncing of sacramental words of the body of Christ, the bread remaineth of the same nature that it was before, neither doth it cease to be bread.' Sautry replied: 'I say that after the pronouncing of the sacramental words of the body of Christ, there ceaseth not to be very bread simply, but remains bread, holy, true and the bread of life. And I believe the said sacrament to be the very body of Christ, after the pronouncing of the sacramental words.' This could be interpreted as consubstantiation: but, in accordance with Wycliffe's teaching, it is certain that Sautry meant that the bread is *sacramentally* the very body of Christ.

The Archbishop probed further 'especially upon the sacrament of the altar'. Sautry somewhat waveringly answered that he knew not whether 'very material bread' remained after the words of the consecration. It was true bread because it was the bread of life which came down from heaven. Asked whether he believed in transubstantiation he replied 'that he knew not what that matter meant'.[47]

After a lengthy examination in which the Archbishop endeavoured to discover his exact views on transubstantiation, Sautry was condemned. He was executed by burning, at the direction of Henry IV. He was the first of the Lollards to be executed in this manner and Foxe attributes it to the desire of Henry to retain the support of the clergy for his seizure of the throne.

John Badby

John Badby, a tailor, of London, was martyred in 1410. In his sentence Archbishop Arundel said that Badby affirmed in his presence 'that after the consecration at the altar, there remained material bread and the same bread which was before; notwithstanding, said he, it is a sign or sacrament of the living God.'[48]

Wycliffe's Wycket

Wycliffite tracts circulated in the fifteenth century. The titles of several appear in the bishops' registers. Of those whose texts have survived *The lantern of Light* treats of the doctrine of the church. The church is a heavenly entity; 'Paradise is holy Church.' It consists of the elect. It is the 'little flock' which Christ speaks of in Luke 12. The tract has only one sentence about the Lord's Supper; 'Judas took the sacrament at Christ's holy supper where Christ dealt his body in bread, as the other apostles did, and drank with them his blood in wine.' The Church authorities of the day regarded this statement as heretical, on the ground that in this statement 'it doth plainly appear that after consecration of bread and wine made, the same bread and wine that was before doth truly remain on the altar.' This was probably the meaning of the author, but a more theologically sophisticated age would hardly have used the adverb 'plainly'!

The most popular of the Wycliffe tracts was one called *Wycliffe's Wycket*. Though full of Wycliffe's ideas, it was probably written by a disciple.[49] It is frequently referred to in the episcopal registers during the fifty years before the Reformation. Thus Foxe relates that in 1518 John Stilman was charged with having received a copy of the *Wycket* about twenty years before, and on his former arrest had hidden the book together with 'one other book of the Ten Commandments' in 'an old oak', but had later recovered the books. Moreover, his indictment went on, he was of the opinion that

'Wycliffe is a saint in heaven and the book called his Wycket is good.' He was burned at Smithfield on October 25, 1518.[50]

From the many references in Foxe, it is plain that *Wycliffe's Wycket* circulated widely amongst the Lollards immediately before the Reformation, that they drew their sacramental doctrines from it, and that it was instrumental in spreading those doctrines.

Though no manuscript of *Wycliffe's Wycket* survives it was printed at least three times in the sixteenth century, in 1546 and twice in 1548. Miles Coverdale was the editor of the second edition, and maybe also of the first. The book deals with the Lord's Supper. It attacks, as the chief error, the worshipping of the host, saying that it is blasphemous to suggest that a creature can make the Creator. Such a doctrine sets up 'an alien God instead of the living God'. Christ's glorified body is in heaven. 'He ascended up very man and very God to heaven and he shall be there till he come to doom the world.'[51]

The bread and the wine is a figure, a likeness, a 'mind' (or reminder) of Christ's body—like a mirror—to bring the reality before the consciousness. 'All the sacraments that are left here in earth are but minds of the body of Christ, but a sacrament is no more to say but a sign or a mind of a thing passed or a thing to come.'[52] This last phrase 'a sign of the thing to come' is interesting but is not developed. For the Lollards, as for the Reformers later, the Lord's Supper does not so much look forward to the messianic banquet in the Kingdom of God as look back to the events of our Lord's life. In the *Wycket,* the bread is primarily a sign of the incarnation and of the reality of his manhood which 'was sustained by food as ours.'[53]

Neither the *Wycket,* nor Wycliffe, have the concept that the sacraments are covenant signs. Nor is the Mass, conceived as a sacrifice, denounced by Wycliffe or the Lollards; indeed the concept appears to be unknown. What is denounced is transubstantiation, as gross idolatry. But in positive exposition of the meaning of the Lord's Supper, the main reformed tenets are already clearly held in the *Wycket* as in Lollardy as a whole.

25

'This is my body'

Wycliffe's Wycket has one interesting exegesis, which does not appear to be in Wycliffe's writings and which is not taken up by the English reformers in general, (though there are occasional echoes of it) but which was accepted by Karlstadt in Germany. This is the explanation that in using the phrase, 'This is my body', Jesus was not referring to the bread in his hand but to his physical body. 'Christ spoke of his holy body when he said, "This is my body which shall be given for you" Luke 22, which was given to death and to rising again to bliss, for all who shall be saved by him. But like as they accused him falsely of the temple of Jerusalem, so nowadays they accuse falsely against Christ and say that Christ spoke of the bread that he broke,.... (They) are deceived, they take it fleshly and turn it to the material bread, as the Jews did to the Temple.'[54] The author went on to say that in the same way, 'This cup' is not a reference to 'the material cup in which he had given his disciples drink' but rather to the suffering he underwent in his body, (which was in fact, how Jesus used the word 'cup' later in Gethsemane, and earlier in his reply to James and John). 'He spoke of his holy body and passion when he said, "This cup is the New Testament in my blood", so he spoke of his body when he said, "This is my body which shall be given for you", and not of the material bread which he had in his hand.'[55]

This same view of the meaning of our Lord's words was held by the Lollard congregation at Amersham. Summarising their opinions (as reflected in the bishop's register), Foxe wrote

...as touching the sacrament and the right doctrine thereof, they had their instruction partly out of *Wycliffe's Wycket,* partly out of the *Shepherd's Calendar,* where they read that the sacrament was made in remembrance of his body, etc. Moreover, they alleged and followed the words of Christ spoken at the Supper, at what time he, sitting with his disciples and making with them his Maundy, took bread and blessed and brake, and gave to his disciples and said, "Eat ye this", reaching forth his arm and shewing the bread in his hand, and then noting his own

natural body and touching the same, and not the bread consecrated, "This is my body which shall be betrayed for you; do this
in remembrance of me".... Item, that Christ our Saviour sitteth
on the right hand of the Father and shall be there unto the day of
doom. Wherefore they believed that in the sacrament of the
altar was not the very body of Christ.[56]

Later Lollardy

It would seem that Lollardy was increasing rather than decreasing at the beginning of the sixteenty century. There is evidence to show how the tenets of Lollardy were propagated in the community. A typical example is the glimpse we get of the life of William Sweeting, recorded by Foxe.

Sweeting held various minor positions of trust in different parts of South East England towards the close of the fifteenth century. It is plain that he witnessed for Lollard truth amongst those with whom he worked. Thus while employed at the priory of St. Osithe's he 'so turned the prior by his persuasions that the said prior of St. Osithe was afterwards compelled to abjure'. When working at Boxted, Essex, first as holy-water clerk, and then as a farmer for a lady land-owner, he had 'much conference with one William Man, in a book which was called Matthew,' to quote the indictment of one of the crimes for which he was later burned. Finally, now an old man, he worked as a cowherd for the town authorities of Chelsea. Here he took the opportunities his work provided of giving religious instruction. Thus, in the trial of James Brewster, a carpenter of Colchester, it was averred by the prosecution, that Brewster 'had been five times with William Sweeting in the fields keeping beasts, hearing him read many good things out of a certain book: at which reading also were present at one time Woodroof or Woodbine, a netmaker with his wife: also a brother-in-law of William Sweeting, and another time Thomas Goodred, who heard likewise the said William Sweeting read.'

Brewster himself was accused of spreading Lollard doctrine, in particular while working with Henry Hert, a fellow carpenter, at Westminster, The bishops' register goes on to record theological discussion on the sacrament 'when Thomas Goodred, William Sweeting and he (Brewster), in the fields keeping beasts were talking together of the sacrament of the Lord's body and like matters'. Both Sweeting and Brewster were burnt at Smithfield in 1511. The grounds of Sweeting's condemnation was that he spoke against pilgrimages and images and because 'he had learned and received of William Man, that the sacrament of the priest's altar was not the present very body, but bread in substance, received in memorial of Christ.'

In the same month that Sweeting and Brewster were executed in London, Thomas Man, another Lollard activist, was tried and abjured by the Bishop of Loncoln's chancellor at Oxford, for, *inter alia,* 'he had denied the corporal presence of Christ's body in the sacrament of the altar.' He was condemned to imprisonment in an Oxford monastery. After some years he escaped and in 1518 he was arrested and tried in London as a relapse and executed at Smithfield. The twelfth and final item of his indictment was 'that in times past he had fled from Colchester to Newbury, and after that into Amersham, and had taught heresies among them: and also, since the time of his abjuration he had said, that he and his wife had turned six or seven hundred people unto those opinions which he was abjured of, and others also, contrary to Christ's faith and determinations of holy church.'[57] From this self-testimony that in the space of seven years one couple had converted hundreds of people to Lollardy, it is plain that England in the early decades of the sixteenth century was readily receptive to Lollard teachings; and it is also plain, from such records as survive that there was no lack of dedicated evangelists of Lollard tenets. At Man's trial, Thomas Risby, a weaver, gave evidence (in Foxe's words) that in the towns west of London there was 'a great company of well-disposed persons, being of the same judgement touching the sacrament of the Lord's supper that he (Man) was of'. At Newbury more than 120 had been forced to abjure and three or four burnt, and the same was true at Amersham, where, although the Lollard congregation was of recent origin, it had grown to a very large size, till Bishop Longland of Lincoln moved against it around about 1521.[58]

An interesting evidence of the intertwining of the influence of Lollard literature and early Reformation preaching in England is the testimony of Thomas Topley in his recantation before the Bishop of London in 1528.

> It fortuned this, about half a year ago that the said Sir Richard went forth and desired me to serve his cure for him; and as I was in his chamber I found a certain book called Wyclif's Wicket, whereby I felt in my conscience a great wavering for the time that I did read upon it and afterwards also when I remembered it, it wounded my conscience very sore. Nevertheless I consented not to it till I had heard him preach and that was upon St. Anthony's Day. Yet my mind was still much troubled with the said book (which did make the sacrament of Christ's body, in form of bread, but a remembrance of Christ's person) till I heard Sir Miles Coverdale preach and then my mind was sore withdrawn from that blessed sacrament inasmuch that I took it then but for the remembrance of Christ's body....[59]

Dr. Peter Brooks has distinguished three viewpoints among historians with regard to the sources in Thomas Cranmer's works, namely that Luther dominated the scene, or that the English Reformers got their sacramental ideas by independent study of the fathers and especially Augustine, or a third view which Brooks put forward as 'a compromise solution' of 'simultaneous discovery', that the English Reformers arrived at their position by their reading at first hand the writings of the continental reformers, along with the fathers.[60] But there is in fact no need to go to the continent for the source of the doctrine reflected in the English Prayer books, for Lollardy had anticipated the full Reformed doctrine. 'None of the English Reformers, with the exception of Robert Barnes agreed with Luther in his belief about the presence of Christ in the sacrament. It was a constant feature in Lollardy to deny the presence of Christ in the sacrament. Thus, an argument used by the Lollards against transubstantiation was repeated by Frith and later incorporated in the Black rubric of the Book of Common Prayer. The teaching of William Thorpe on the nature of Christ's presence in the sacrament, that he is received by faith into the heart of the faithful Communicant, is identical with that later expounded by Frith and Cranmer.'[61]

The doctrine of the Lord's Supper as expressed by the English Reformers is fully anticipated in the surviving records of Lollardy, scrappy though these are. For example, in 1485 the Bishop of Coventry and Lichfield examined Robert Crowther who was accused of holding 'that whoso receiveth the sacrament of the altar in deadly sin or out of charity, receiveth nothing but bread and wine.'[60] This is identical with the doctrine of Article 29 of the Thirty-nine Articles. The wording of the accusation shews that Crowther believed that those who came rightly to the sacrament received more than bread and wine, i.e., they received the body and blood of Christ. These two concepts (that the believer receives only bread and wine but the believer truly feeds on Christ) together epitomise the Reformed doctrine of the Lord's Supper. Another example of Lollard anticipation of Reformed doctrine of the Supper is the doctrine that Thomas Beele of Henley taught Elizabeth Stanford about the year 1506, namely, that 'the sacrament of the altar is not the very body of Christ but very bread: and that the sacrament was the very body of Christ put upon the cross, after a divine and mystical manner.'[63] Christ is received through His Word, believed in faith and obeyed. '...the holy sacrament, Christ's own body: this is not received by the chewing of teeth but by hearing with ears, and understanding with your soul and wisely working thereafter.'

Luther ridiculed the concept that Christ's body was shut up in heaven, as though Christ was a bird in a cage. However, this concept (without Luther's imagery!) was typical of Lollardy and of the English Reformation. Thus shortly after he was promoted to the bishopric of London in 1522 Tunstall compelled Edmund Spilman, a priest, and three others 'to abjure and renounce their professed faith touching the holy sacrament of Christ's body and blood; which was that Christ's corporal body was not in the sacrament, but in heaven, and that the sacrament was a figure of his body and not his body itself.'[64] In 1508 Elizabeth Sampson was abjured for believing that the sacrament was 'bread, for that Christ could not be both in heaven and in earth at one time'.[65]

Many Lollards suffered martyrdom rather than renounce their faith. Foxe records the steadfastness of Laurence Chest, 'who was burned at Salisbury for matter of the sacrament in the days of Henry VII', in the presence of his wife and seven children who were brought for the purpose of persuading him to recant.[66] These public spectacles of faithfulness must have had a powerful effect on those who witnessed them or heard of them and doubtless contributed to the spread of Lollard conviction in England immediately before the beginning of the Reformation on the continent.

In 1521, after Luther had been excommunicated, but before the Reformation had overtly begun in England, Bishop Longland of Lincoln prosecuted scores of humble folk living in the Cotswold villages. The process was a cruel one in as much as suspects were required under oath to accuse their neighbours and themselves. Parents were compelled to accuse children and children parents, and spouse to accuse spouse. On conviction, they were required to abjure their opinions and were then sentenced as penitents to lifelong imprisonment with hard labour in a monastery sustained by such alms as they were given. Those who had been convicted on a previous occasion were publicly burnt, their children being compelled to light the fire.[67]

Early Reformers

One of the first of the English reformers to write on the Lord's Supper was George Joye. He composed his treatise towards the end of 1532 but publication of his book was delayed. Willian Tyndale (who is the source of this information) did not know whether the reason was lack of money or inability to find a printer. In the meanwhile, Sir Thomas More published an attack on the Reformers' doctrine although nothing had yet appeared in print. This was dated 7th December, 1532. The occasion of More's attack was a handwritten copy of a letter by John Frith on the Lord's Supper, which had been sent to More by one of his spies. Indeed, since obtaining his first copy More said that he had been 'offered since a couple of copies more in the meanwhile whereby men may see how greedily these new named brethren write it out and secretly spread it abroad.'[68]

The importing of English books printed beyond the sea had been prohibited, and More suggested that this was the reason the 'heretics' were composing short books capable of being copied by hand. However, they manage 'in their treatises to put as much poison in one written leaf as they printed before in fifteen'! Frith's original letter has not survived but what the Reformer's opinions were may be gathered from the Lord Chancellor's confutation of them.

More recognised that Frith's doctrine of the Lord's Supper was not drawn from Luther, but rather from Wycliffe,

Oecolampadius, Tyndale and Zwingli. 'He runs a great way beyond Luther...affirming it not only to be the very bread still, as Luther does, but also as those other beasts do, says it is nothing else, and that there is neither the blessed body of Christ nor His blood, but, for a remembrance of Christ's passion only base bread and wine, and therein goeth he so far in conclusion that he says it is all one unto us whether it be consecrated or unconsecrated.'[69]

More affirmed that Frith stood out beyond all former heretics in making so little of the consecration. 'He maketh in manner (taking the consecration so slight and so light) no manner sacrament at all, wherein he runneth yet beyond Tyndale and all the heretics whatever I remember before.'[70] Frith's opinion that consecration was immaterial was the natural consequence of the return to the doctrine that the bread and the wine are only signs, sacraments, 'visible words' of the gospel of the grace of Christ. Consecration by the priest, which was so essential in the doctrine of transubstantiation, did not have the same significance in the Reformed doctrine of the Lord's Supper. Consequently Frith is quoted by More as saying that one need not be troubled whether the sacrament is consecrated or not because 'the priest cannot take from us the fruit of God's instruction.'[71]

More said that Frith's teaching was that Jesus' words, 'This is my body', ought not to be taken literally since in other places Jesus called himself a true vine and a door. 'Not for that he was in all these things indeed but for certain properties for which he likened himself to these things', just as Jacob called the altar 'the God of Israel' and the place of his wrestling 'the face of God' and just as the paschal lamb was called 'the passover'. 'As the paschal lamb was a token and remembrance of the passing by of the Lord and as a bridegroom giveth his bride a ring if he hap to go into far country from her for a remembrance of him in his absence and as a sure sign that he will keep her his faith and not break her his promise.'[72] In this last simile it is clear that Frith regarded the Lord's supper as a covenant sign given by Christ to his people on the eve of his departure. It was a sign to recall to mind his faithfulness.

Frith argued that our Lord's word, 'This is my body', cannot be taken literally as Christ's body cannot be in two places at once. But More replied that all things are possible with God.[73] God can make Christ's body to be in all places at once. 'God is almighty and therefore can do all things.... This young man hath yet in his youth gone too little while to school to know all that God can do.'[74]

It would seem that Frith had composed a liturgical prayer to be said by the congregation before receiving the sacrament. Had this survived it would have been the earliest English Reformed liturgy. More, however, did not think much of it. 'And as for that holy prayer that this devout young man as a new Christ teacheth to make at the receiving of the blessed sacrament all his congregation, I would not give the parring of a pear for his prayer.'[75]

George Joye

Shortly after More's attack on Frith appeared, it was answered by a book entitled 'The Supper of the Lord', and dated the 5th April, 1533. No author's name was attached and although More's informers told him it was by George Joye, More himself was not certain, and it has been frequently ascribed to Tyndale. However, the content and style confirm that Joye, and not Tyndale, was the author.

One of the most interesting features of this book is the order for celebrating the Lord's Supper with which it concludes.[76] This is the first English Reformed liturgical order. The church polity envisaged is congregationalism under the godly prince—bishops presumably are to be a thing of the past. The prince should appoint 'over each parish such curates as can and would preach the word'. The Lord's Supper is to be celebrated 'once or twice in the week'. The emphasis is on the corporate fellowship character of the rite. It is the congregation who are the body and blood of Christ (quoting St. Paul's phrase) and the service is 'preaching the Lord's death' and an exhortation to trust and thankfulness for this.

The congregation respond to the curate's exhortation, each one contributing—'everyone, some singing, and some saying devoutly, some or other psalm or prayer of thanksgiving, in the mother tongue.' At the time of receiving the bread and the wine, the congregation is to gather round 'the pastor exhorting them to pray for grace, faith and love which all this sacrament signifieth and putteth them in mind of.' The sign is the action of the service. Then the bread and wine will be distributed to the congregation, 'every man breaking and reaching it forth to his next neighbour and member of the mystic body of Christ, other ministers following with the cups, pouring forth and dealing them the wine, all together thus being now partakers of one bread and one cup, the thing thereby signified and preached printed fast in their hearts'.[77]

The service concludes with a thanksgiving for the benefit and death of Christ, 'Whereby now by faith every man is assured of the forgiveness of his sins; as this blessed sacrament hath put them in mind and preached it them in this outward action and supper.' This done, let every man dedicate himself to God and return home.

Joye stressed the dimension of thanksgiving in the Supper. 'Christ said... this thing do ye into remembrance of me, that is to say, so oft as ye celebrate this supper, give thanks to me for your redemption.'[78] Joye wished to revive the name 'the thanksgiving', for the service. It was a thanksgiving for redemption as was the passover.[79]

For Joye, the concept of the supper as a fellowship activity was vivid. But, though Joye appreciated the fellowship of the supper, it is a fellowship of our redemption rather than our hope. Joye (and this is true of all the English Reformers) saw the Supper as backward looking; quoting, 'They drank of the stone which went with them, which stone was Christ', he commented: 'They believed in Christ to come, we believe in him comen and having suffered.'[80] The concept that the Supper was also a sacrament of the Messianic banquet and the Christian hope is absent from the writings of the English reformers of this period.

Like Frith, Joye had no place for the concept of consecration in the service. He pointed out that the words, 'This is my body, this is my blood', which the theologians took as words of consecration were spoken by Jesus after he had commanded the bread and the wine to be eaten and drunk and after the disciples had obeyed. So any such consecration was much too late, as the elements were no longer in our Lord's hands and had indeed already been consumed![81] In combating the doctrine of transubstantiation, Joye cited St. Paul's words, 'As often as you eat this bread', adding, 'Lo, this heretic calls it bread, even after the words of the Pope's consecration.'[82]

He charged his opponents with inconsistency in standing pat on the literal sense of 'This is my body', but recognizing the symbolic in the phrase, 'This cup is the New Covenant', and instanced many biblical examples of the copula 'is' meaning 'stands for' such as 'the three baskets are three days', and, 'The seven fat oxen are seven pleantous years.'[83]

In this book Joye was very conscious of the fellowship features of the Supper. 'By the thanksgiving (for so did old Greek doctors call this Supper), at God's board, or at the Lord's Supper, (for so doth Paul call it) we testify the unity and communion of our hearts, glued unto the whole body of Christ in love: and that in such love as Christ at this his last supper expressed. To be short, as baptism is the badge of our faith, so is the Lord's supper the token of our love to God and our neighbours.'[84] (*Ibid* 246).

The concept of fellowship based on the death of Christ was in the foreground of his thought again when he quoted 1 Cor. 10:16: 'The cup of thanksgiving which we receive with thanks is it not the fellowship of the body of Christ? The bread which we break, is it not the fellowship of the body of Christ?'[85] and in commenting on the phrase, 'guilty of the body and blood of the Lord,' Joye wrote: 'The body and blood of the Lord, Paul called here the congregation assembled together to eat the Lord's Supper, for they are his body and blood which are redeemed by his body and blood'.[86]

The character of the Lord's Supper as fellowship was not a concept that was stressed by other English Reformers. However, it was prominent in Joy's thinking. Indeed, in his edition (August 23, 1534) of Tyndale's New Testament, most of which he reproduced without change, he altered (following Erasmus' paraphrases) Tyndale's translation (1526) of 1 Cor. 10:16. Tyndale had translated: 'Ys not the cuppe of blessings

37

which we blysse, partetakynge of the bloude of Christ? Ys not the breed which we breake partetakynge of the body of Christ?' For this, Joye substituted: 'Ys not the cuppe of thankisgeving which we blysse the felowship of the bloude off Christ? Is not the bread which we breake the fellowship of the body of Christ.' And in the *Supper of the Lord* he expounded this thus: 'Paul calleth the cup of thanksgiving 'the fellowship of the blood of Christ', that is to say, the congregation redeemed with Christ's blood'. 'Of the bread, (Paul says) "Is it not the fellowship of the blood of Christ?" That is to say, "doth it not signify to us to be the body of Christ; that is his congregation and people?"'[87]

The above comment is interesting, not only for its understanding of the meaning of the supper, but even more so, for the doctrine of the Church. Joye defined the congregation as a fellowship redeemed by Christ's blood, and interpreted 'the body and blood of Christ' as a term defining the congregation.[88]

Joye maintained his translation of 1 Cor. 10:16 as 'fellowship' in his edition of January 9, 1535, as did Tyndale his of 'partaking' in the 'New Testament yet once again corrected ....' of 1535.

Both Matthew's Bible (1537) and Taverner's (1539) followed Tyndale identically (except for spelling) as also does Coverdale (1535), except that he followed Joye in the opening phrase 'the cuppe of thanksgiving wherewith we give thanks....'

Erasmus, in his paraphrase on 1 Cor. 10:16 had already written:

> Doth not that holy cup, which we with thanksgiving consecrate and receive in remembrance of Christ's death, declare a fellowship that we all are delivered through the death of Christ? Doth not again likewise that holy bread which we, as Christ both gave example and commanded break among us, show a special league and fellowship betwixt us...?'

Erasmus published his paraphrase in Latin in 1516 following the issue of his New Testament. Translated by Coverdale and others they were published in English in 1549.

John Frith

A few months after Joye's book on the Sacrament was published there was also published a book on the same subject by John Frith, written while a prisoner in the tower. It was an expansion of his letter which Thomas More had answered. Frith was martyred in July 1533 and his book on the Lord's Supper was published shortly afterwards. In it he deals first with Christ's presence in the sacrament. The Lord's supper expresses that relationship with God through faith in Christ in which our salvation consists. That relationship may be described through the metaphor of eating and it is a relationship essentially the same under both covenants. Of Abraham, Frith wrote: 'We shall be saved if we eat Him (Christ) spiritually as he did!'. Following St. Paul, he argued that the ancient Israelites shared with Christians an identity of religious experience. They ate and drank the same spiritual food, namely Christ. This disposed of the doctrine of Transubstantiation. 'They were never so mad to believe that the manna was changed into Christ's own natural body but understood it spiritually that as the outward man did eat the material manna, so did the inward man, through faith, eat the body of Christ... and likewise do we eat Christ in faith, both before we come to the sacrament, and more expressly through the sacrament and with no less fruit after we have received the sacrament.'[89]

The above quotation brings out two features of Frith's theology of the sacrament which were characteristic of the English reformers. These two features are firstly, the concept of what may be called 'double eating', that as we eat the physical elements with our mouth, we also eat, if faith is present, the body of Christ in the soul; and secondly, the concept that feeding on the body of Christ in the sacrament is not different from our feeding on Christ as the bread of life in other ways, though the Sacrament may be described, as Frith here does, as a 'more express' way. This is because it focuses faith more expressly. There is no grace of a special kind associated with the Lord's Supper.

This raises the question of why we celebrate the Supper.

Frith asked: 'Here thou wilt object against me.... [that if faith without this sacrament be sufficient] what needeth the institution of a Sacrament?'[90] This is a pertinent question (which the reformers never staisfactorily answered, with the exception of Joye, who understood the sacrament primarily as a fellowship meal in thanksgiving).

Frith gave three reasons for the institution of the Sacrament of the Supper:

1. Sacraments serve as a badge to integrate the Christian community. 'There can no congregation be served out of the multitude of men but they must needs have a sign token sacrament or common badge by the which they may know each other and there is no difference between a sign or a badge and a sacrament but that a sacrament signifieth a holy thing and a sign or a badge doth signify a worldly thing. St. Augustine says 'Signs when they are referred to holy things are called sacraments.'[91]

(The modern reader should note that the Reformers always used the word sacrament to mean sign. For them sign and sacrament were synonymous words. When they speak of a sacrament they mean a sign and when they say 'sacramentally' they mean 'by way of a sign'.)

2. The second reason for the institution of sacraments is to move us to faith by the truth being 'expressed to divers senses at once.' Frith instanced the case of a man who shakes hands after receiving an agreement verbally. 'He counteth that this promise is strong and more faithful because it moves more senses.' So Christ gave bread the name of his body and commanded it to be eaten to impress the truth of their redemption through his crucified body the more strongly on the disciples' minds, 'that even as that bread doth nourish the body so doth faith in his body breaking nourish the soul unto everlasting life.'[92]

3. The third reason is that the Supper should be an opportunity to publish the gospel to others and to give thanks before the congregation.

These three arguments of Frith make the sign the purpose of the Lord's Supper. But actually it is the activity which is the true centre. This activity is fellowship—fellowship with

Christ and with one another on the basis of the gospel, that is, the basis of forgiveness of sins and the hope of glory in Christ. The sign—the eating and drinking of bread and wine designated Christ's body and blood—is the word of the gospel, the basis of the fellowship, and faith in this word is the response which is itself the fellowship with Christ, and so with one another in Christ. Thus so long as the Lord's Supper is seen primarily as a sacrament, that is, a sign, there is difficulty in justifying it over against the preached word, as Frith found; but if it is seen as primarily an activity of fellowship around the word and the response to that word, the sacrament requires no justification, as fellowship is an end in itself.

Frith came near to the concept of the supper as a fellowship activity when, like Joye, he translated *koinonia* in 1 Corinthians 10 as 'fellowship'. 'Paul calleth it bread saying, "The bread which we break, is it not the fellowship of the body of Christ?"'. In this translation Frith did not follow the printed edition of his friend Tyndale's New Testament, where the passage reads: 'Is not the bread which we break partaking of the body of Christ'—quite a different meaning. Frith was conscious of the Christian fellowship which the partaking together of the Lord's Supper expressed. It was its use in the context of joyful fellowship which made the bread of the Supper different from ordinary bread. 'The bread and the eating of it in the place and fellowship where it is received is more than common bread. What is it more? Verily it is bread which by the eating of it in that place and fellowship doth testify openly unto all men that he is our very God whose cup we drink and before whom we eat in that fellowship and that we put all our affiance in him....'[93] It is not only a fellowship activity between the believer and Christ but also between believers one with the other. 'When we come together to receive this bread, then by the receiving of it in the congregation we do openly testify that we all which receive it are one body.'[94]

Frith distinguished between our Lord's use of the term 'body' for the bread, and St. Paul's use of 'body' for bread. 'Christ did call himself bread and here St. Paul calleth us

41

bread.... As St. Paul calleth the bread our body, for a certain property, even so doth Christ call it his body for certain other qualities.'[95]

As a consequence of this exegesis Frith is able to bring a further argument against the doctrine of transubstantiation. 'In this they agree' (that is to say, Paul and Christ), 'that as Paul's words must be taken spiritually (for I think that no man is so mad as to judge that the bread is our body indeed, although in that property it represents our body) even so must Christ's words be understood spiritually.'[96]

Frith is the clearest and most forceful, as well as the earliest expositor of the doctrine of the Sacraments amongst the Reformers. In spite of attempts to make out that Frith held a doctrine of the real presence in the elements, nothing could be clearer than that Frith is a Sacramentarian. Thus he grounds the reverence due to the Sacrament solely on the ground of the solemn doctrine that it teaches. He could not have done this had he believed in any presence associated with a sacramental bread and wine, for then this would have been the pre-eminent reason for reverence.

We give it (the sacrament) the same honour which we give unto the Holy Scripture because it expresses unto our senses the death of our Saviour and doth deeply imprint it within us. And therefore we call it an holy sacrament as we call God's Word, Holy Scripture, and we receive this sacrament with great reverence even as we read and hear preached the Holy Word of God which contains the health of our souls and we grant that His Body is present with the bread as it is present with the Word and with both it is verily eaten and received through faith.[97]

It is clear that he did not associate our Lord's body locally with the elements.

Frith's sacramentarianism is also abundantly clear in his lengthy comparison of the passover eaten in Egypt and the Lord's supper eaten in the Upper Room.

The paschal lamb was very lamb indeed and so is the sacrament very bread indeed.... They that believed the Word of the Lord did more eat the passing by of the Lord which should deliver

them than they did the Lamb. They that believed the Word of
the Lord did more eat the body of the Lord which should be given
for their deliverance than they did the bread. For that thing
doth a man most eat that he most hath in memory and most
resolveth in mind, as appeareth by Christ (John 4): "I have meat
to eat that ye know not of." They that believed not the next day
to be delivered from Egypt did not eat the passing by of the Lord,
although they did eat the lamb. They that believed not the next
day to be delivered from sin, did not eat the body of the Lord.
though they ate the bread.[98]

There is absolutely no difference between Frith, Joye and
Tyndale (or for that matter between these three and Ridley
and Cranmer who wrote later) with regard to their belief
about the relationship of the bread and wine and the presence
of our Lord's body. The relationship is that of a sign to the
reality. The presence of our Lord's body in the elements is a
sacramental presence, that is, presence by way of a sign only.
There was no difference between the English Reformed
writers on the Lord's Supper with regard to the doctrine of
the presence of Christ in the sacrament. All were Sacra-
mentarians.

Many modern writers in anxiety to align the English
Reformers with current Sacramental theology fall into the
trap of failing to distinguish between realism and realistic
language. All biblically based doctrines of the Lord's Supper
must use realistic language, for our Lord himself used it
when he took bread and said, 'This is my body.' The mere
quotation of realistic language does not in itself resolve the
question how the language is to be understood. Luther at
Marburg failed to see this and he has been followed by
numerous controversialists both Roman and Anglo-Catholic.
The English Reformers were aware that the use of realistic
language by the Early Fathers did not in itself imply a belief
in the real presence, any more than our Lord's use necessarily
implied realism with regard to the presence in the elements.
They also affirmed that the believer was entitled to use
realistic language in regard to his participation in the sacrament and that to seek to avoid it merely showed lack of faith.
Thus Frith wrote:

We say that they speak well and faithfully which say that they go to the body and receive the body of Christ and that they villainously and wickedly which say that they only receive the bread of the sign of his body, for in so saying they declare their infidelity.... The faithful will think that he is ill reported of... if men should say of him that he did only receive the sacrament and not also the thing which the sacrament doth signify. For albeit he only eateth the bread and sacrament with his mouth and teeth yet with his heart and faith inwardly he eateth the very thing which the sacrament outwardly doth represent.[99]

At his interrogation by the Bishop, two questions were put to him. The first was on purgatory.

The second was thus, whether I thought that the sacrament of the altar was the body of Christ, and I said that I thought it both was the body of Christ and also our body as St. Paul says in 1 Corinthians 10...well, said they, do you not think that his very natural body both flesh and blood is really contained under the sacrament and these actually present beside all similitudes. No, saith I, I do not so think....

Frith added:

The cause of my death is this because I can not in conscience abjure and swear that our prelates' opinion of the Sacrament (that is, that the substance of bread and wine is verily changed into the flesh and blood of our Saviour Jesus Christ) is an undoubted article of faith necessary to be believed under pain of damnation. I will not bind the congregation of Christ (by my example) to admit any necessary article beside our Creed and especially none such as can not be proved true by scripture.[100]

William Tyndale

About this time William Tyndale wrote *A brief declaration of the sacraments*. Since he dealt with both baptism and the Supper together under the concept of sacrament he had little scope for treating the Supper as a fellowship *activity*. In fact, this concept is absent and Tyndale reverted exclusively to the concept of sign. The Supper, like baptism, is a preached word. 'As the Hebrews wrote their stories in covenants and signs [Tyndale gave a list of these]...even so Christ wrote the covenant of his body and blood in bread and wine...and hereof ye see that our sacraments are bodies of stories only, and that there is none other virtue in them than to testify and exhibit to the senses and understanding the covenants and promises made in Christ's blood.'[101] In particular, the Supper preaches the forgiveness of sins and so is a way 'to seek absolution', i.e., the assurance of forgiveness. 'The sacrament is an absolution of our sins as often as we receive it where it is truly taught, understood and received aright.'[102]

Neither baptism nor the Supper is absolutely necessary. 'Our salvation does not stand in that or in any other sacrament, that we could not be saved without them by the preaching of the word only.' However, 'God hath written his will to have his benefit kept in mind, to his glory and our benefit.' The sacraments are words conveying the message of the gospel in outward signs and actions. They are suited to our nature and God in his grace has provided them for our assistance. As a hen clucks for her chicks, so God gathers his children, weak in faith, to him by this sacrament.[103]

With regard to the question of the real presence of Christ in the elements, Tyndale insists that we must interpret idioms according to the custom of each language. 'We have a thousand examples in the Scriptures where signs are named with the name of the thing signified by them as Jacob called the place where he saw the Lord face to face, Pheniel, that is God's face...though it was not his very face.' Thus our Lord's words, 'This is my body', must be interpreted according to the idiom of the language to which he and his hearers were accustomed.[104]

Tyndale answered the Lutherans who appealed to the language of the Fathers to support the doctrine of the real presence by reminding them that the Fathers also called the supper a sacrifice, which the Lutherans denied. The correct interpretation of the Fathers, according to Tyndale is that in both matters they call the sign by the name of the thing signified. The Fathers called the supper a sacrifice because it was 'the memorial, the earnest and seal' of Christ's sacrifice on Calvary, and they 'called the sacrament the body and blood of Christ after the same manner only, because it is a memorial, earnest and seal of his body, and blood, as the use of the scriptures is to call signs by the names of the things signified thereby.'[105]

The papists continually argued that the Reformers' denial of transubstantiation was due to a failure of faith in the almighty power of God, but Tyndale replied that 'the almightiness of God standeth not in that He is able to do all that our foolish lewd thoughts may imagine.'[106] However, he was willing to tolerate the term transubstantiation in that in the supper bread and wine 'cease to be any more bread and wine in the hearts of the believers; for the heart, after the words once spoken, thinketh only of the covenant made in the body and blood of Christ.'[106] This seems identical with the doctrine of transignification espoused by some Dutch Roman Catholic theologians and obliquely condemned by Pope Paul VI in his encyclical MYSTERIUM FIDEI. Tyndale wrote his book in Holland, so Holland has seen the theological wheel come full circle!

John Lambert

Frith and Tyndale both suffered martyrdom under Henry VIII. A third to suffer in this way was John Lambert, who was burnt for denying the doctrine of transubstantiation in 1538. Before his death he wrote a book giving reasons for his views, which was edited and published by John Sale in 1548. In it Lambert acknowledged that the bread and wine are rightly called the body and blood of Christ. Indeed he was willing to call them the true natural body of Christ, because Christ only has one body, so that whatever may be called his body may be called his true natural body. Nevertheless, Lambert felt the need for clarity's sake to qualify his acknowledgement by the phrase 'after a certain manner'. 'I grant the Holy Sacrament to be the very and natural body of our Saviour and the natural body and blood of our Saviour is in the sacrament after a certain manner.'[108] What this 'certain manner' was he later explained.

Our souls...into whom nothing corporal can corporally enter, doth not carnally receive the body and blood of our saviour, neither did He ordain His blessed body and blood so to be eaten and drunken, although our souls cannot live except they be spiritually fed with the blessed body and blood of Him, spiritually eating and drinking them, in taking also at times convenient the blessed sacrament which is truly called his body and blood. Not that it is really but...because it is a sign or figure of Christ's body and blood. And the sign or sacraments doth commonly...take their denomination of the things by them represented and signified.[109]

For if the sacrament had not a certain similitude of those things of which they be sacraments then should they not be sacraments at all. By reason of which similitude they do for the most part receive the denomination or name of those things signified and therefore after a certain manner the sacrament of Christ's body is the body of Christ and the sacrament of Christ's blood is the blood of Christ and also be the sacrament of faith called faith.[110]

Lambert devoted a considerable section of his treatise to showing that our Lord's body could not be in two places at one time without contradicting scripture and destroying the reality of our Lord's manhood. The scriptures, the Fathers and the Creeds unite in affirming that our Lord's body is in heaven and is coming again at the end of the world. If it is said that it is still in the world in the sacrament, 'It should then be both to come and already come, which is a contradiction and a variant of his manhood.'[111]

'A Declaration of the Seremonies...'

In 1537 a little book of 14 pages appeared entitled 'A Declaration of the Seremonies a nexid, to the sacrament of Baptysme, what they sygnyffie and how we ought to understande them.'

The anonymous author described the ceremonies of baptism in order to stress the necessity of 'the second baptism', that is, the converted sanctified life under the influence of the Spirit, which these ceremonies signify. It was to this second baptism that John the Baptist referred when he contrasted his water baptism with the baptism of the Spirit and fire,

> and without this second baptism may no man be saved, as Christ said to Nicodemus...also Paul teacheth that the first baptism in water only maketh us not safe but the asking of a good conscience in God.... That man that shall dwell before the face of God in heaven shall receive the earnest of the Holy Ghost here in earth. And this is the second baptism which fleshly priests and swinish people knoweth not.... Priests be in peril that teach not the second baptism.[112]

It is interesting to note that the author recognised that the true meaning of baptism of the Spirit is relationship to Christ through the Spirit's indwelling experienced by all who are converted to Jesus as Lord.

Matthew's Bible

In 1537 Matthew's Bible was published by Royal Licence and set up in churches. It incorporated as a preface a short theological word-book in which the Lord's Supper was defined thus: 'The supper of the Lord is a holy memorial and giving of thanks for the death of Christ'. Under the word 'sign' there is this comment: 'Christ has left us two signs for to shew and protest our faith before his church, that is to say, the water of baptism, Mar 16d, and the bread and wine of his holy supper, Mt. 26c.'

Richard Taverner

In 1539 Richard Taverner translated (without acknowledgement) Calvin's *Instruction in Faith* published in French in 1537. In general Taverner translated Calvin faithfully, but in the sermon on the Lord's Supper, he made some interesting variations, which reflected the political and theological situation of English Reform in 1539. Conforming to the Act of Six Articles, Taverner listed seven sacraments, and omitted Calvin's express denial of the Real Presence. But more interesting is his expansion of Calvin's text to stress typical English Reformed viewpoints. Calvin's semi-mysticism is dispersed by easily understood concepts. The bodily eye which sees the signs and figures of bread and wine is contrasted with 'the inward eye of faith' which sees 'how the Lord gives the true partaking of his body and blood.' Taverner stressed that Christ is now in heaven, slightly expanding Calvin at this point, and he glossed Calvin's comment that 'Christ nourishes his own with himself' to make clear that this means having personal fellowship with Christ here and now. 'For although he being now taken up into heaven, keepeth his residence in heaven and no longer on earth, I mean in presence and human likeness, yet no distance of place can let [= hinder] him to feed his faithful with his own self and so to work that they (though heaven and earth be never so far assunder) should yet have most present fellowship and company with him.'[113]

Taverner followed Calvin in the definition of a sacrament. 'A sacrament is therefore properly an outward sign wherein God represented and witnessed his goodwill towards us to sustain the weakness of our faith.'[114] Sacraments are for the purpose of exercising our faith 'before God and men'.

The purpose of the Lord's Supper is 'to acertain us, that the Lord's body was once so offered, so betrayed for our sakes that now it is ours, yea and ever more shall be and that his blood was so sprinkled and shed for us that it should be ours for evermore.[115]

Catholic Reaction

Joye's 'Frutefull Treates...'

In 1539 The Act of Six Articles—the bloody whip with six cords, as it has been called—strictly forbade denial of transubstantiation. However, George Joye published anonymously *A frutefull treates of baptyme and the Lord's Supper* in 1541. This book contains a full exposition of the doctrine of the sacraments as signs of God's promises (i.e., of his covenant). It would appear to be a source book of the doctrine reflected in the Edwardian Prayer-books. The sacraments were instituted by God 'to stir up our senses that the things promised by the words might the more presently and deeply be conveyed unto our hearts and minds' (p.1). Joye defined a sacrament thus: 'A sacrament is an outward sensible sign whereby God declares and certifies to the worthy receivers thereof his good mind, benevolence and favour to us: whereby also he sustains and helps the weakness of our faith.'[116]

There are only two sacraments, and these are 'badges and cognizances of the christian society and fraternity'. 'The use or action...of these sacraments, do exercise our faith and makes us the more assured of his good will towards us.'[117]

Joye emphasised the need for communicants to examine themselves before they took part in the Lord's supper. He quoted Augustine that the unworthy receiver eats or drinks not the body and blood of Christ, 'but only the sacrament of so great a thing.'[118]

The sacrament speaks to us of Christ's death for our forgiveness. There is a double seeing: 'We see with our bodily eyes the holy bread broken...but with the eye of faith... Christ's body broken and his blood poured forth for the remission of our sins...and given us.'[119] There is a double eating, of which the consequence is that Christ dwells in our heart by faith. 'Our souls thus eating him by faith, have Christ present and He is in us by grace, governing us by His Holy Ghost.'[120]

The bread is Christ's body sacramentally, that is, by way of a sign (sacrament and sign being synonymous). That which is 'verily, really and naturally' Christ's body is that which was crucified on Calvary (and is now in heaven).[121]

Though 'young infants and men bestraught' are members of Christ's body, yet they are not suitable subjects to receive the Lord's Supper, 'for these persons may not rightly remember the mystery of their redemption, nor duly examine and prove themselves before, nor give thanks therefore, which things are chiefly required at the celebration of this holy feast.'[122]

Joye concluded his treatise with a lengthy exposition of the necessity of examining oneself before joining in the Lord's Supper. He condemned his opponents in this respect. 'This just probation as our papists never practised it in themselves, so never yet taught it they their flocks.'[123] When Paul told us to discern the body before partaking of the Supper, this implies that we are to examine ourselves to see whether our life indicates that we are in truth members of Christ's body.[124]

The distortion of the supper into the mass, and errors in its administration such as the withholding of the cup, are also, in Joye's judgement, forms of unworthy reception of the Supper, and in particular they are 'guilty of the blood of Christ who feed not their flock with the food of God's Word.'[125]

Zwingli

Another book attacking transubstantiation which appeared in English during this period of Catholic reaction was a translation by George Joye[126] of Zwingli's *Reckoning and declaration of faith*. Perhaps it was because it was a document which had been presented to the Diet of Augsburg of 1530 that the anonymous printer was emboldened to publish it in English in 1543.

In this book Zwingli with great ability expounded his theology under twelve heads. In number eight he dealt with the Lord's supper. He begins: 'I believe that in the holy supper of thanksgiving the very body of Christ is present.' However, it 'is present to the eyes and contemplation of our faith'. Rejecting both transubstantiation and Luther's consubstantiation, Zwingli explicitly denied 'that the very natural body of Christ either should be essentially corporally or really in the supper or eaten with our mouths or teeth in the form of bread as the papists dream or in the bread as some men imagine which yet sit and look back unto and for the pots full of flesh out of Egypt.'[127]

The celebrating of the sacrament is the confession of our faith.

> It is through the manhood of Christ that our sins have been atoned for, so that when the bread is made a sign of Christ's body, this is the acknowledgement that we are saved through his death. They that give thanks unto the Lord for that benefit given us in his Son acknowledge Him to have taken unto Him very manhood, [i.e., as we give thanks in the sacrament we acknowledge the reality of the Lord's incarnation] In it verily to have suffered, and verily to have had taken away our sins in His blood and so everything done by Christ to be as it were present unto them at the eyes and contemplation of their faith.[128]

Zwingli's view of the sacrament of the Lord's Supper is at one with that of the English reformers and with Calvin. They were united in their views on the contentious question as to Christ's presence in the sacrament, and also on the nature of the grace of the sacrament. Christ's body is present in the sacrament, but present sacramentally, that is, by way of sign. And it is the body of Christ—Christ in his crucifixion, when he gave Himself for the life of the world—that is present by way of sign. Secondly, in the Supper there is a double eating, 'the sacramental eating' and 'the spiritual eating', for just as the body is nourished by the bread and wine, so the soul through faith eats the bread of life. Zwingli has no place in his thought for the concept of a mere bare remembrance commonly attributed to him, for a bare remembrance can only mean a remembrance without faith or thanksgiving—a possibility open only to the unregenerate or carnal Christian!

The unity of Zwingli's views with those of his fellow Reformers is clear when he writes:

> The old doctors and divines did always speak significantly when they attributed so much unto the eating of the body of Christ in the Supper, that is to wit, not that the sacramental eating might purge the soul but faith in God through Jesus Christ, which is the spiritual eating did purge it, of which faith and spiritual eating, these outward things are the significance and shadow. And as the corporal food sustains the body, as doth wine refresh it and make it glad, so doth that faith stablish our mind with the blood of Him when our faith certifieth us that our sins which so burned our conscience be quenched by His blood.[129]

In this book presented to the Diet of Augsburg, Zwingli concentrated much of what he had to say about the sacrament in disproving transubstantiation, as well as consubstantiation. He pointed out that Christ's words, 'Me ye have not always', do not apply to Christ's divine presence but can only refer to his manhood, (of which his body was an integral aspect) while to maintain the ubiquity of Christ's human body 'were to take away the very manhood of Christ, for nothing may be everywhere but the Godhead.'[130]

Henry Brinkelow

Besides Joye, there were other authors who published on the Lord's Supper during the reaction of Henry's last years. Henry Brinkelow wrote *The lamentation of a christian man against the city of London* in which he denounced the mass. 'The supper of the Lord... is turned into a vain superstitious ceremonial mass (as they call it) which mass is become an abominable idol and of all idols the most greatest.'[131] Brinke-low argued that the notion of the Real Presence in the Lord's Supper contradicts the nature of a sacrament. 'Thou sayest it is a sacrament, which I both grant and write. If it be a sacrament as it is in deed, then it is a sign of some holier thing than it is itself, so can it not be God, for what sign or token wilt thou have holier than God.'[132]

Brinkelow highly commended the writings of John Frith on the Lord's Supper. 'John Frith...has written invincibly in this matter...and I exhort you in God's name, if there be any christian printer in London, to print more of those works, for there can never be too many of them. Fear not, man, though death follow, seeing Christ saith, He that loseth his life for my sake shall save it.'[133]

William Turner

On September 14th, 1543 William Turner, a vigorous controversialist, published in Basle *The hunting and fyndynge out of the Romishe fox*. It was an attack on the continued use of the canon law in England as contrary to the action of the king who had excluded the Pope's laws from England. Turner kept within the Six Articles but complained of certain erroneous doctrines and practices which were still continued. 'Ye hold still that a priest may receive the sacrament of Christ's body and blood for a layman and that the layman's sins may be taken away by the priest's receiving for him...ye hold still that by the mass...ye can deliver damned souls out of hell.' The sacrament is also received 'for measled swine,...for the French pox'.[134]

Turner concluded by saying that he had just heard that the bishops had made a law confining the reading of the Bible to gentle folks, which he denounced as discrimination between the rich and the poor in the matter of salvation.

John Lassels

John Lassels, a member of the King's service, was burned at Smithfield on July 16th, 1546. Before his death he issued a

Protestation, which seems to have had a wide circulation. He and his companions had been questioned on the effect of the words *Hoc est corpus meum*—'This is my body.' Lassels maintained that Jesus alone could say these words and that by them he was referring to his death on Calvary which fulfilled them. Lassels distinguished between the supper in the upper room which was unique and fulfilled at Calvary and the Emmaus supper which is the prototype of the Lord's Supper. In his exposition of the Lord's Supper, Lassel's followed normal English reformed theology, but has some phrases which found an echo later in the Book of Common Prayer. 'When the bread is broken acording to the ordinance of Christ the blessed and immaculate lamb is present with the eyes of our faith and we eat his flesh and drink his blood, which is to dwell with God and God with us and in this we are sure that we dwell with God in that he has given us His Holy Spirit.'[135]

Lassels emphasised that the wicked do not eat Christ's body, for it is 'belief which maketh the presence of Christ'. Otherwise the devil could not have entered into Judas who 'received the same wine and bread which the other apostles did'. However for the priests to make Christ's presence in the bread is to do more than Christ did.

Miles Coverdale printed Lassels' *Protestation* as an addendum to his corrected edition of *Wycliffe's Wycket* which he published in 1547. In his preface he said that many had taken Lassels to say 'that Christ speaking these words [*Hoc est corpus meum*] pointed to his body which suffered on the morrow.' This was a view propounded by Andreas Bodenstein Von Karlstadt, a former colleague of Martin Luther. But it was not a view that found support among the English Reformers. Coverdale commented that such an 'assertion as it is voided of all wit and learning so it is contrary to the true meaning of the words of this godly man'. It is a scheme of the devil to promote such a view among believers 'that all the world shall have them in contempt and derision'. Moreover, it takes away the sacrament altogether, for if Christ did not speak these words of the bread, to make them a sign of his body as a sacrifice in which we are all partakers 'what should we do with it more than common bread. How should we certify our conscience withal if Christ had spoken nothing of it?'[136]

Luther

Toward the end of the Catholic reaction a small book was published (with a plainly false colophon) entitled *The disclosing of the Canon of the popish mass, with a sermon annexed unto it of the famous clerke of worthy memory D. Martyn Luther.* The anonymous editor in the preface speaks of God's judgement of 'sword, famine and pestilence' from which England was suffering. This may be a reference to the same national calamities, to deprecate which Cranmer wrote the English litany. With a reference to the Catholic reaction, the translators asked their readers to recognise 'the abomination of idolatry shamefully used in these days and not only used but with force and main fortified and upholden with fire and faggot, cruelty and strength and was so sore upholden that the eternal word of God is clearly banished, exiled and put to death'.[137] Luther's doctrine of Consubstantiation found little support in England. None of the writings of the English Reformation endorse it but are consistently opposed to it and they all without exception favour the theology of Switzerland. This is doubtless due to the teaching of Wycliffe and the Lollards which the English Reformation inherited. However, Luther's attack on the mass as a propitiatory sacrifice was enthusiastically taken up in England, of which this book is an example. Luther's sermon began by setting out salvation by the grace of Christ, then proceeded through the canon paragraph by paragraph, denouncing and ridiculing the concept of sacrifice that had been grafted on to it. For example, Luther commented on the action of the priest who before the consecration offers the bread with a prayer that it might be accepted as a sacrifice: 'Here standeth a wretched brainless man at an altar and like a fool asketh that he may make an acceptable, a holy and untouched sacrifice when he hath nothing but a morsel of bread and a sip of wine...Darest thou, a man, sinful and worms meat, stand forth in the sight of God's majesty and before Him play the fool with a piece of bread and a little wine.'[138] After the elements have been consecrated and so (on Roman theory) have become the body and blood of Christ, the priest in the Canon prays that they may be as acceptable as was Abel's sacrifice. Luther commented: 'Is the blood of Christ of no more value than to be compared to Abel's oblation, a young lamb?' Abel himself had been saved by Christ's sacrifice. 'Here now they pray to God to take it as acceptable as he did Abel's sacrifice, even as though Christ were inferior to Abel.'[139]

The old religion defended

Towards the end of Henry VIII's reign two learned defenders of the old religion entered the literary fight against the reformed doctrines. Stephen Gardiner, Bishop of Winchester, wrote a book of 312 pages entitled *A Detection of the Devil's sophistrie wherewith he robbed the unlearned people of the true belief in the most blessed sacrament of the aulter.* Gardiner relied heavily on authority, quoting extensively from the fathers. Thus in confuting the reformers' argument that St. Paul called the sacrament bread he wrote: 'Hath not the church had and understood these words of Scripture which ye so vehemently allege? Hath not the church delivered these words unto us? And hath not the same church notwithstanding taught this truth, how the bread by consecration is converted into the precious body of Christ?'[140] In a similar way the Church condemned the Arians who said that the Father is greater than the Son, notwithstanding the words of Scripture 'The Father is greater than I.' Repeating an argument found on page 61 of Henry VIII's book against Luther, *Assertio Septem Sacramentum,* Gardiner quoted the example of Aaron's Rod—which the Scripture still called a rod after it had been turned into a serpent.[141] However, Gardiner added, faith does not need these arguments.[142]

The other defender of the established doctrine was Richard Smith, the first Regius Professor of Divinity at Oxford and later to be the first principal of the seminary at Douay. He published two books in 1546/7. Both were lengthy. The first was entitled *The Assertion and Defence of the Sacrament of the Aulter.* Smith was scandalized both by the egalitarian democracy of the reformation, and by the many forms of literature which were used to disseminate the doctrine.

> In time past... it was not in any way sufferable, that tag and rag, learned and unlearned, old and young, wise and foolish, boys and wenches, master and man, tinkers and tylers, colliers and coblars, with such rascabalia might at their pleasure rail and jest... not sparing any sacrament of the church... in so much that both by preaching and teaching (if it so ought to be called), playing, writing, printing, singing and (O good Lord) how many other ways is, divers of our age, being their own school masters or else scholars of the devil, have not foreborne nor feared to speak and write against the most excellent and most blessed sacrament of the altar that it is nothing else but a base figure and that there is not in the same sacrament the very body and blood of our blessed Saviour and redeemer Jesus Christ, but only a naked sign, a token, a memorial, and a remembrance only of the same, if they take it for so much and do not call it (as they be wont to do) an idol, and very plain idolatry.'[143]

It was to correct all this that Smith wrote his book.[144] He began with a short summary of his doctrine: 'That in the said most blessed sacrament of the altar by the strength and efficiency of Christ's most mighty word, it being spoken by the priest, there is present really under the form of bread and wine, the natural body and blood of our saviour Jesus Christ, conceived of the Virgin Mary, so that after the consecration there remaineth no substance of bread and wine nor any other substance, but only the substance of Christ, God and man.'[145] The book ran to 260 folios and was divided into four sections: an exposition of Catholic doctrine; rules for true understanding of doctrine; notable errors in the past; present-day objections and their solution. More than half the book is taken up by this last section, which itself is divided into two. The first is devoted to Frith's objections, of which Smith lists 26, and the second to 47 other current objections. It is interesting that Smith should give such prominence to Frith, which is an indication of the ongoing influence of the latter's book, some fifteen years or so after his death. (It is equally interesting that neither Gardiner nor Smith includes Tyndale in the list of heretics whose writings had to be avoided). Smith objected to Frith's method of arguing the matter in that he dispensed with authorities and simply argued from the nature of the case![146] Smith's second book, *A defence of the sacrifice of the Mass,* is an answer to Luther's sermon. Although it is 189 folios, Smith in his preface said that 'it was made in haste, in the space of a month.'[147] Smith argued that since Hebrews 5 states that priests are chosen from among men to offer sacrifices, 'This text is manifestly against Martin Luther's heresy that all Christian people are priests', and secondly: 'Since every priest has to offer some sacrifice', Smith concluded, 'no man can well deny but that the mass is a sacrifice.'[148] The preface is dated July 20, 1546. In it Smith records his pleasure that 'the King's Majesty, like a most solemn prince, has put forth a proclamation of late straightly charging and commanding that no man or woman do keep after the last day of August next ensuing any book in English that contains in it any ill or hurtful doctrine.'[149] But within six months the King was dead.

The Reign of Edward VI

A. Gilbey

The new reign brought a relaxation of inhibitions for author and printer. Within a few days of Edward's succession a detailed answer to Stephen Gardiner by A. Gilbey was published. It was a book of 430 pages. In reply to Gardiner's authoritarianism, Gilbey began by insisting: 'The Lord our God is a God of knowledge.... It becometh all His to labour for knowledge that they may walk upright in the way of the Lord and by no halting ignorance to slide forth of the same and so provoke His worthy displeasure.'[150] The Sacrament is addressed to our reason; but to believe in transubstantiation is to live with 'the act of magic'. 'God hath appointed his Holy word to be preached to us reasonable creatures, and the more especially in this sacrament... so that it is overmuch shame to use Christ's word as an enchantment over dead creatures,' 'The receiving of the sacrament is the preaching of the death of Christ.'[151] Christ gave the Supper for remembrance of Him. This implies that he is absent in body. 'That ye should make God in remembrance of God in my opinion is against reason. I may say, and rail not, it is a mad heresy.'[152] We feed our souls in the Supper through the gospel (which is the only meat of the soul) 'that they increasing in full faith of God's mercy (which is the life of the righteous) may be nourished, grow and increase to the full age of a perfect man in Christ Jesus.'[153]

It will be noted that Gilbey speaks of our feeding ourselves by dwelling on 'the truth of the Gospel'. Other writers preferred to say that God feeds us through our apprehension of the promises exhibited in the sacrament. But though the phraseology differs, the meaning is identical.

William Turner

William Turner, the author of *The hunting and fyndynge out of the Romishe fox,* was by profession a medical man and his work on English herbs is famous. In his preface to *A New Dialogue wherein is conteyned the examination of the masse* (1550), Turner excused a physician's writing on theology by the analogy that every citizen, however unskilled in war, is called on to defend his city when threatened. He designated the Sacrament as 'the most comfortable common seal of our liberty and redemption.' But the papists 'in the stead of the same set in a mere man's invention, a certain popish play which they call the Meritorious Mass.'[154] The Mass is not the Lord's Supper, instituted in the scriptures, for the objects of the two services are different. The Mass is offered to make satisfaction for sin, and 'to heal sick horse, measled swine.' Turner quoted the words of the requiem to disprove the quibble that the mass is only offered for remission of temporal and not eternal punishment. 'In this prayer is plain mention of deliverance from hell, without any figure or trope. "Lord Jesus Christ King of Glory deliver the souls of all faithful dead from the hand of hell and the deep lake."'[155]

The object of the Lord's Supper is quite different. 'The end of Christ's Supper is to remember Christ's death, to give thanks for our redemption and to remember that we are all members of one body and ought therefore to love one another.'[156]

Turner crusaded against vestments and stone altars. 'The vestments, for all the bishop's babblings, are no holier than Tom Tinker's taberd is, and the name of God is abused, when it is called upon to sanctify things God never commanded to be sanctified or hallowed.'[157] As for altars, Turner wrote 'The Sacrifices that are allowed of Christian men to be offered are these, The calves of our lips, prayers, thanks, praising God, charitableness and mercy and alms to the poor, our own bodies mortified, a contrite heart and a troubled spirit. I pray you now, what shall we need an outward and a stone altar to offer these sacrifices on? Then when we need no such altars it is evil done of you to hold still altars in the Church, whereas Christ's table should be. Now your altars do none other good but bear false witness against Christ that He hath not made perfect all that are sanctified with his blessed sacrifice. For an outward altar presupposeth an outward sacrifice, but another outward sacrifice for sin after Christ's presupposeth that Christ's sacrifice was not sufficient or perfect enough, for St. Paul to the Hebrews proveth that the sacrifice that hath another succeeding is imperfect.'[158] Turner therefore concluded that altars 'ought to be broken down and taken away.' It is interesting to note that within a few months the authorities gave orders that this should be done.

Thomas Broke

More than twenty-five books on the Sacrament were printed in English in 1548, the first full year of Edward's reign. Notice can only be taken of one or two of them here. Thomas Broke, a prominent citizen of Calais and Dover, wrote a small book twice published in 1548 entitled *Certyn Meditations and thinges to be had in remembraunce and well considered by every Christian before he receive the sacrament of the body and bloud of Christ'*. In it Broke affirmed that the sacraments strengthen faith through our reasoning.

'All sacraments, (both of the Old and New Testaments) were instituted of God to put us in remembrance of His most loving benefits... which benefits these sacraments through God's word do offer into our mind and not to our senses and we receive the same benefits by faith into our souls and not with our senses into our bodies.'[159]

Broke affirmed a real absence of Christ's human body. The New Testament references to the (second) coming of Christ are 'spoken of one that is absent, and not of one that is present, wherefore, doubtless, Christ's natural body is absent, in heaven, and not present in a corporal presence in the Sacrament of the Altar,'[160] Nevertheless we feed on Christ's natural body in the Sacrament, for if we believe Christ's natural body and blood was crucified for us as depicted in the Sacrament 'we then eat Christ's natural body and blood in spirit and faith to our everlasting life, although we believe not any manner of transubstantiation... The spiritual eating of Christ's body is to believe in Him.'[161]

The Christian is united with Christ in heaven now. He is 'one with our Head Christ and in heaven with Him', for he is in his mystical body.[162]

Broke was the first translator of Calvin's *Institutes*. Only a part of what he translated was printed, namely chapters 6 to 10 of Book Three. He tells us in his preface that he translated a good deal more of it but presumably the troubles in Mary's reign prevented it from being printed and what happened to it afterwards is not known. Broke's translation is more vigorous and idiomatic in style, more anglo-saxon and less latin in vocabulary than that of Thomas Norton who produced the first complete translation of the Institutes in Elizabeth's reign.

John Calvin

Calvin's *Treatise on the Lord's Supper,* translated by Miles Coverdale (who had published the first complete edition of the English Bible in 1535), was printed about this time. In his preface Coverdale gave his reason why the Supper is called the body and blood of Christ. It is because Christ's death is its message. 'The most Sacred Sacraments also of the body and blood of Christ are called His body and blood because they declare unto us what the body and blood of Christ be unto us, none otherwise than I call this book the Supper of the Lord, because it declareth the Supper of the Lord.'[163] Christians, on the other hand, are called the body of Christ because they were purchased by his body. As one may buy an article for one hundred pounds and say, 'That is my hundred pounds', so we having been bought by the sacrifice of Christ's body may be called his body. Such is Coverdale's explanation of St.

Paul's terminology.

Calvin began his book by stating that the Treatise is intended to be 'a summary of what is necessary to be known of the Lord's Supper'.

Calvin stated that the Supper is an attestation of the word, which is the source of our spiritual life. 'The bread is called the body because it not only represents but also presents it to us...the name of the body of Jesus Christ is transferred to the bread inasmuch as it is the sacrament and figure of it.'[164] Calvin stressed the necessity to be a partaker not only of Christ's spirit but also of his humanity 'in which he rendered all obedience to his Father in order to satisfy our debts, although properly speaking, the one cannot be without the other.'[165] We may partake of Christ through the sacrament, for receiving the body is always the result of receiving the bread, because of the reliability of God's character.[166]

It will be seen that Calvin regards the Supper as primarily an individual means of grace.

Calvin denounced any local presence.

> To wish to establish such a presence as is to enclose the body within the sign or to be joined to it locally is not only a reverie but a damnable error. As our Lord took our humanity, so he exalted it in heaven, withdrawing it from mortal condition but not changing its nature'. 'To fancy Jesus Christ enclosed under bread and wine, or so to conjoin him with it as to amuse our understanding there, without looking up to heaven, is a diabolical reverie.'[167]

It is extraordinary that in spite of these statements the editor of this treatise, in his Introduction to his translation in the 'Library of Christian Classics' edition (Vol. 22) wrote that in it Calvin taught 'a true and real presence of Christ in the elements'.[168]

The body of Christ is not present in the elements but in heaven. Calvin put the matter clearly: 'The Lord Jesus gives us in the Supper' (note: in the Supper, not in the elements) 'that which he signifies by it and consequently we truly receive the body and blood of Jesus Christ. Nevertheless he is not to be sought as if he were enclosed under the bread or attached locally to the visible sign. So far from adoring the sacrament believers will raise their understanding and their hearts on high, as well to receive Jesus Christ as to adore him.'[169]

Calvin concluded his treatise by denying that there was any difference in doctrine on the Supper between himself and Zwingli and Oecolampadius. This contemporary testimony that there is no such thing as Zwinglianism, by someone who was not a Zwinglian, ought to be decisive. Of course Calvin was right, for 'Zwinglianism' is a figment of the imagination. A 'bare remembrance' of Jesus is possible only to the unregenerate or the carnal Christian. No spiritually-minded believer can remember the Lord without at the same time being in conscious fellowship with him through the Spirit, so that a 'bare' remembrance is impossible, while genuine remembrance is fellowship with Christ, than which no higher blessing is possible. Thus the Supper, being a means of remembrance, is a true means of grace. Calvin and Zwingli, together with the English reformers, were united on the doctrine of the sacraments, and of the Lord's supper in particular, though different writers stressed different aspects. Of Zwingli and Oecolampadius Calvin wrote: 'Being so bent on opposing the superstitions and fanatical opinion of the papists touching the local presence of Jesus Christ within the sacrament and the perverse adoration consequent upon it, that they laboured more to pull down what was evil than to build up what was good. For though they did not deny the truth they did not teach it so clearly as they ought to have done. I mean that in their too great anxiety to maintain that the bread and the wine are called the body of Christ because they are signs of them, they did not attend to add, that though they are signs the reality is conjoined with them and thus protest that they had no intention whatever to obscure the true communion which the Lord gives us in His body and blood by this sacrament.'[170]

William Punt

On December 17, 1548 a small book was published, written by William Punt, entitled *A new dialogue called the endightment against mother messe.*

This book is a dialogue between Verity, Wisdom, and Mass. It takes the form of a court room scene. Verity and Wisdom indict Mass of treason and murder. The twelve apostles are empanelled as the jury; God's Word sits as judge. The verdict goes against Mass on the ground that 'Paul says in the letter to the Hebrews that we are sanctified by offering up of the body of Christ once for all.'[171] Consequently, she has betrayed Christ as did Judas, and has murdered 'Richarde Hunne, Robert King, John Debenham, Nicholas Marsh, Thomas Saxte, Thomas Hitton, Thomas Bilney, Richard Bifield, W. Tewkesbury and Colyns, William Leton, George Bainham, John Frith, John Lambert, William Tyndale, Robert Barnes, William Gerard and Jerome and 500 more'.[172]

Verity argues that since scripture says, 'Christ became in all points like unto man, saving sin, now I reckon that one man's body can be but in one place at one time. It therefore could not be in the disciples' mouths when it was sitting at the table with them, nor in the mass when it is now in heaven.'[173]

Mass replies, 'Why sir, God is omnipotent', and therefore can do it. Since he says, 'This is my body,' we should accept that.[174]

The reply to this is that God has said that he does not dwell in temples made with hands, while transubstantiation implies that he does.

Mass is condemned, but the judge allows her liberty 'till the parliament be done'. Then she is to be banished out of the land.[175]

On the last page this aphorism is appended: 'A true proverb ... the nigher the church the further from God. (Quod.) W.P.'

Also this poem:

'You subjects of baal, say what you will

66

Kick, spurn and winse, as much as you may,
Make as many gods as you can it will not skill
That at length without doubt you shall want you play.'

The Debate of 1548

Towards the end of 1548 the Protector Somerset required the bishops of the Church of England to dispute whether 'bread be in the sacrament after the consecration or not'. The debates took place in the House of Lords in December 14–18, 1548. A condensed report of the debate has survived. The most remarkable feature of the debate is the clearness with which all the reforming bishops denied any reception whatever of the body of Christ by the wicked. The report of the debate makes clear that the 1549 Prayer Book reflects the same eucharist doctrines as does the 1552 book. In the debate both Ridley and Cranmer affirmed the absence of the reality of Christ's body in the elements. Bishop Heath asked 'whether the receiver taketh any substance in the sacrament or not?'[176] Ridley replied: 'The carnal substance sitteth on the right hand of the Father. After this understanding of the presence he is not in the sacrament, for he saith he will leave the world...The manhood is ever in heaven. His divinity is everywhere present. ...Christ sits in heaven and is present in the sacrament by His working.'[177] Similarly Cranmer saith: 'Our faith is not to believe him to be in the bread and wine, but that he is in heaven.' Tunstall replied: 'His body is in bread and wine, because God hath spoken it, which is able to do it', but Ridley said: 'The question is not whether he might do so or not but whether he has done so or not.'

Cranmer stressed the double eating. 'They be two things, to eat the substance and to eat the body of Christ. The eating of the body is to dwell in Christ, and this may be though a man never taste the sacrament. All men eat not the body in the sacrament.' Cranmer described transubstantiation as a comfortless doctrine 'for as soon as you tear the body with your teeth (they say) the body flies to heaven, for it may suffer no such wrong, and while it is in the bread we have not comfort...'.

Bishop Heath asked Ridley whether there was any change in the substance of the bread after consecration. Ridley's reply was that there was no change in the substance of the bread but there was a change in the action effected by the use of the bread. It became a communion of the body of Christ to the faithful but death and a judgment to the wicked.[178] So too Cranmer: 'Christ when he said This is my body, he meant "Communion of my body". For Christ, when He bids us eat His body, it is figurative. For we cannot eat His body in deed.'

Was Cranmer inconsistent?

Cranmer has been accused of vacillating in his doctrine of the presence of Christ in the Supper. Thus C. W. Dugmore believes that he changed his views day by day in the Parliamentary debate.[179] D. G. Selwyn says there was a shift earlier in 1548 between the second and third editions of his translation of Justin Jones's Cathechism[180] (the first edition was in June, the third in August 1548); while others again think he changed his views between the 1549 Prayer Book and the 1552 book.

The evidence for such variation is illusory. Cranmer himself stated that he had held only two views of the presence of Christ in the sacrament,[181] that is, the old view of transubstantiation and the reformed or Zwinglian view which he adopted shortly before publishing the first edition of the Catechism. The variations which modern writers discover between the other reformed writers is equally illusory.

What these critics have not sufficiently considered is the problem inherent in realistic language. At the Last Supper Jesus took bread and said 'This is my body.' For those who believe in a real presence this presents no problem of language. The bread becomes the body. But for those who like the Reformers believe that Jesus was speaking sacramentally, that is, figuratively, there is an ongoing problem of language whenever the bread is spoken of. Thus it is correct to say that we eat with our mouth the body of Christ; and (once the question of realism is raised) it is equally correct to say that we do not eat with our mouth the body of Christ. This dual form of stating the truth must be used by all who believe that Jesus said, 'This is my body', with regard to what the disciples were eating and yet do not believe that Jesus implied thereby a real presence of his body in the sacrament. To deny the logical possibility of this dual form of statement is tantamount to affirming that the doctrine of the real presence is the only possible interpretation of our Lord's words, 'This is my body.' Reformed theologians use one form of words in one context to stress one aspect of the truth, the opposite form of words in another context to correct fatal misunderstanding of the sacrament. But modern writers treat this variation as vacillation, which of course, it is not.

In talking about the Lord's Supper reformed theologians used language which has two levels of meaning, for this is scriptural; but this is not the same as ambiguous language. Reformed exegetes maintain that there is no ambiguity in our Lord's words taken in their context of the Last Supper. Ambiguity is never a virtue; like lying, it is a misuse of language and is to be eschewed. Theologians, like all who use words, must strive for clarity of expression.

In the third edition of Justin Jones' Catechism, as well as in the Second Prayer book, Cranmer altered the language to make it unmistakably reformed. This is not to say that the former language was less reformed (Cranmer himself strongly denied this accusation) but rather that the former expressions had proved to be less clear than they should be in an area where Cranmer was anxious there should be no ambiguity.

Realistic language must always be used of the Lord's Supper in order to do justice to the truth of our forgiveness and incorporation in Christ through his death in his human body, but realism, i.e., the concept that our Lord's body is present in substance and not in figure or sacrament only, is rejected without equivocation in all the writings of the English Reformation. Realistic metaphorical language, standing by itself, cannot be distinguished from the language of literal realism, but requires for its true interpretation qualifying or alternative statements. It follows that the statements about the supper in the English Reformers and in the church formularies should be allowed to interpret one another and not be taken as indications of vacillation or conflict in doctrine; for the Reformers, holding the views that they did about the Lord's Supper, could not avoid the use of alternations in language. Indeed, when the reformers did so, they were following the usage of Scripture, which speaks both of bread and of the body of Christ.

Notes

1. The Eucharist, 2.9. (*On the Eucharist'*, John Wycliffe, edited and translated by Ford Lewis Battles, Library of Christian Classics, Vol. XIV. *Advocates of Reform* (SCM Press) 1953)
2. Ibid. 8.1
3. *Trialogus* p.135 (*Trialogus,* John Wycliffe, translated by Robert Vaughan, *Tracts and Treatises of John de Wycliffe,* London 1845) Cf. *The Eucharist. op. cit.* 2.10
4. *Trialogus, op. cit.* p.140
5. Ibid. pp. 145 f. cf. *The Eucharist, op. cit*
6. *Trialogus, op. cit*
7. Ibid. p.143
8. Ibid. p.142
9. *The Eucharist, op. cit.* 1.9
10. Foxe Vol. IV, p.667 (*Acts and Monuments,* John Foxe edited by Josiah Pratt, London 1877)
11. *Trialogus, op. cit.,* p.133
12. Ibid. p.134
13. *The Eucharist, op. cit.,* 1.11
14. *Trialogus* (Ed. Vaughan) p.139
15. Ibid. p.148
16. Ibid. p.148
17. Thomas Cranmer succinctly stated these three points. 'all that love and believe Christ himself, let them not think that Christ is corporally in the bread but let them lift up their hearts to heaven and worship him sitting there at the right hand of his Father. Let them worship him in themselves whose temples they be in whom he dwelleth and liveth spiritually; but in no wise let them worship him as being corporally in the bread, for he is not in it, neither spiritually as he is in man; nor corporally, as he is in heaven; but only sacramentally as a thing may be said to be in the figure, whereby it is signified.

71

'Thus it is sufficiently reproved the third principal error of the papists, concerning the Lord's Supper, which is that wicked members of the Devil do eat Christ's very body, and drink his blood' *The Defense of the True and Catholic Doctrine of the Sacrament,* Book IV chapter XI.

18. *Trialogus* (Ed. Vaughan)
19. *The Eucharist* (Ed. Battles) 4.18
20. Ibid. 4.18 cf. Thomas Cranmer 'Christ as concerning his body and his manhood is in heaven' *op. cit.* Book III chapter III
21. *Trialogus* (Ed. Vaughan) pp.132, 152
22. *The Eucharist* (Ed. Battles) 1.15
23. Ibid.
24. Ibid. 1.17
25. Ibid. 1.15
26. Ibid. 4.21
27. Ibid. 1.7 For the concepts of 'double eating' and 'the eye of faith' in the reformers, cf. Thomas Cranmer 'As with our corporal eyes, corporal hands, and mouths, we corporally see, feel, taste, and eat the bread and drink the wine, being the signs and sacraments of Christ's body, even so with our spiritual eyes, hands and mouths, we do spiritually see, feel, taste and eat his very flesh and drink his very blood.' *op. cit.* Book IV chapter VIII; cf. also John Jewel: '...the eye of our soul, which is faith' 1 Jewel 540 (Parker Society edition).
28. Ibid. 1.11
29. *Trialogus* (Ed. Vaughan) p.148
30. *The Eucharist* (Ed. Battles) 1.14
31. Ibid. 2.10 cf. Article XXV of the Thirty-nine Articles.
32. Ibid. 4.44
33. Ibid. 4.43
34. Ibid. 1.14
35. Ibid. 4.38
36. D. B. Knox: *The Doctrine of Faith, in the reign of Henry VIII* (James Clarke, 1961) p.33
37. *The Eucharist* (Ed. Battles) 4.38
38. Ibid.
39. Ibid.
40. Foxe *op. cit.* III.132
41. Ibid. III.109
42. Ibid. III.174
43. Ibid.
44. Ibid.
45. Ibid. III.175
46. Ibid. III.204
47. Ibid. III.222
48. Ibid. III.237
49. H. B. Workman: *John Wycliffe* 11.39n
50. Foxe, *op. cit.* IV.207

51. *Wycliffe's Wychet* (R.T.S. Edition) p.164
52. Ibid. 162
53. Ibid. 164
54. Ibid. 158
55. Ibid. 165
56. Foxe *op. cit.* IV.241
57. Ibid. IV.211
58. Ibid. IV.213
59. Ibid. V.40
60. P. Brooks: *Thomas Cranmer's Doctrine of the Eucharist—an Essay in Historical Development* (Macmillan, 1965) P.XV ff.
61. D. B. Knox: *The Doctrine of Faith, in the reign of Henry VIII* (James Clarke, 1961) p.94.
62. Ibid. IV.133
63. Ibid. IV.205
64. Ibid. IV.174
65. Ibid. IV.125
66. Ibid. IV.126
67. Ibid. IV.245
68. *The Works of Sir T. Moore* (Ed. 1551) p.833A
69. Ibid. 833B
70. Ibid. 834
71. Ibid. 842
72. Ibid. 834
73. Ibid. 839
74. Ibid. 841
75. Ibid. 844
76. Tyndale: *Works* (Parker Soc.) III 265
77. Ibid. III.267
78. Ibid. III.242
79. Ibid. III.242, 245
80. Ibid. III.244 81. Ibid. III.241
82. Ibid. III.251
83. Ibid. III.249
84. Ibid. III.246
85. Ibid. III.255
86. Ibid. 87. Ibid. III.264
88. Ibid. III.267
89. *A Boke made by John Frith prisoner in the Tower of London, answering unto T. More's letter* (1533) A5b
90. Ibid. A8
91. Ibid. A8b
92. Ibid. B1
93. Ibid. J8a
94. Ibid. J7a
95. Ibid. J6

96. Ibid. J7
97. Ibid. L1b
98. Ibid. L4b
99. Ibid. L1
100. Ibid. L6b
101. Tyndale: Doctrinal Treatises (Packer Soc. I) 358
102. Ibid. I.357
103. Ibid. I.360
104. Ibid. I.368
105. Ibid. I.371
106. Ibid. I.380
107. Ibid. I.372
108. *A Treatise made by John Lambert unto King Henry VIII* fol. 23
109. Ibid. fol. 30
110. Ibid.111. Ibid. fol. 22b
112. *A Declaration of the Seremonies a nexid, to the Sacrament of Baptysme* fol. 5
113. *A Catechism... set forth by Richard Taverner* p.68
114. Ibid. p.64b
115. Ibid. p.68
116. *A Fruitful Treatise of Baptysm and the Lord's Supper* p.2
117. Ibid. p.3
118. Ibid. p.12
119. Ibid. p.6
120. Ibid. p.7
121. Ibid. p.11
122. Ibid. p.13
123. Ibid. p.14
124. Ibid. p.17
125. Ibid. p.25
126. J. F. Mozley in *Notes and Queries* 185 (1943) p.252
127. *The Reckoning and Declaration of faith and belief of Huldrich Zwingli* C 3f (1548)
128. Ibid.129. Ibid. D.1b f
130. Ibid. C4
131. *The Lamentation of a Christian Man against the City of London* A7
132. Ibid. C
133. Ibid. C1b
134. *The hunting and Fyndynge out of the Romishe fox* p.14
135. *Protestation of John Lassels* C1
136. Ibid. B6
137. *The disclosing of the Canon of the popish mass A2b*
138. Ibid. B5b
139. Ibid. C2
140. *A detection of the devil's sophistry* fol. 119b
141. Ibid. fol. 115b

142. Ibid. fol. 118
143. *The Assertion and Defense of the Sacrament of the Aulter* fol. 3b, f
144. Ibid. fol. 5
145. Ibid. fol. 14
146. Ibid. fol. 90b
147. *A defense of the Sacrifice of the Masse* fol. 15
148. Ibid. fol. 69ff
149. Ibid. fol. 14b
150. *An answer* fol. 2
151. Ibid. fol. 36
152. Ibid. fol. 26
153. Ibid. fol. 35ff
154. *A New Dialogue* A2
155. Ibid. C5
156. Ibid. D2
157. Ibid.158. Ibid. F5b, ff
159. *Certeyne Meditations* A2
160. Ibid. A7b
161. Ibid. B2
162. Ibid. B7
163. *A faithful and godly treatise* B2b
164. *Short treatise on the holy supper of our Lord Jesus Christ* (translated by Beveridge, Calvin Tracts Vol. II Edinburgh 1849) §15
165. Ibid. §13
166. Ibid. §16
167. Ibid. §42
168. Page 140, Introduction, *Treatise on the Lord's Supper*, John Calvin, edited and translated by the Rev. J. K. S. Reid, Library of Christian Classics Vol. XXII *Calvin: Theological Treatises* (SCM Press 1954)
169. Ibid. §51
170. Ibid. §158
171. *A new dialogue* B2b
172. Ibid. B4
173. Ibid. B6
174. Ibid. B6b
175. Ibid. C2
176. J. T. Tomlinson: *The Great Parliamentary Debate in 1548 on the Lord's Supper*, London (1895) p.14.
177. Ibid. p.38
178. Ibid. p.50
179. C. W. Dugmore: *The Mass and the English Reformers* London (1958) p.129.
180. *Journal of Theological Studies* Vol. 15, pt. I (1964) p.83
181. cf. J. I. Packer, *The works of Thomas Cranmer* (1964) p.xvi